Basic Truths
of the Christian Faith

by

r. j. arthur
under shepherd, teacher, author, lecturer, student

Published by the P.A.C. of America

Basic Truths of the Christian Faith

Copyright © 2001 by R. J. Arthur. All rights reserved; however, all materials can and should be copied, reproduced, and/or used as often as possible for other's spiritual gain, but may not be copied, reproduced, and/or used for any financial gain.

ISBN: 978-1496106971

All scripture quotations, unless otherwise indicated, are taken from ESV Bible® (The Holy Bible, English Standard Version®). Copyright © 2001 by Crossway, a publishing ministry of Good News Publishers. Used by permission. All rights reserved.
Printed in the United States of America

Basic Truths
of the Christian Faith

by

r. j. arthur
under shepherd, teacher, author, lecturer, student

_____
name

Table of Contents

Title Page	page i-iv
Table of Context	page v
Course Prospectus	page vi
Preface	page vii
How to Use the FAQ Section	page viii
FAQ of the Christian Faith	pages 1-42
Session 1, *The Bible*	pages 43-47
Session 2, *The One True God*	pages 48-53
Session 3, *God the Father*	pages 54-57
Session 4, *God the Son*	pages 58-61
Session 5, *God the Holy Spirit*	pages 62-65
Session 6, *Satan*	pages 66-71
Session 7, *Humanity*	pages 72-75
Session 8, *Salvation*	pages 76-123
Session 9, *The Christian Life*	pages 124-129
Session 10, *The Church*	pages 130-137
Session 11, *The Ordinances*	pages 138-149
Session 12, *The Second Coming*	pages 150-155
Session 13, *The Future Life*	pages 156-162

Course Prospectus

Subject:

- Thirteen basic truths of the Christian faith

Books and Materials:

- The *Basic Truths* workbook

- The ESV® Study Bible (i.e. English Standard Version)

The Basic Truth Study Objectives:

- To encourage self-discipline with *daily reading* and *daily studying* of the scriptures.

- To learn how to use the tools found in the ESV Study Bible (i.e. cross-references; footnotes; commentary notes; maps; charts; concordance; etc.).

- To develop the proper method of interpretation in order to "handle accurately the word of truth."

- To provide deeper insight into the basic truths of the Christian faith in order to develop one's personal relationship with God through Jesus the Christ.

- And possibly most important, all of the above objectives are designed to be easily reproduced from one disciple to another. Obedience to Jesus Christ is the greatest objective. Jesus has commanded us to make disciples. This study is designed as a discipleship tool so believers can pursue obedience. Every disciple that goes through this study will be able to take other future disciples through this study, and then teach them to obey by doing the same, and so on, and so on.

Preface

Truth

What Is Truth?
What is Truth? Truth is defined in the Webster Dictionary as "that which is true; a fact; a reality; that which conforms to fact or reality; the real or true state of things." There are various categories of truth. For example, there is mathematical truth (i.e. 2 + 2 = 4); scientific truth (i.e. gravity); personal perspective truth (i.e. the type of foods one may like); and spiritual truth (i.e. God created everything). Each of these various categories has their place of importance. Each of these categories also has their own path or methods for pursuing truth and confirming their fact or reality.

The Importance of Spiritual Truth
Spiritual realities affect every person. The fact of the matter, whether people know it or not, is that every person will stand before the God of the Bible and give an account for how they lived their life here on earth. But the importance of Spiritual Truth is deeper than personal interest. Spiritual Truth is important because God is important. Those who love God will desire to get to know God. The reason those who love God want to know Him is to better understand what is important to God in order to better obey Him. The Bible says if you love God you will obey Him. The only way to obey God is to know His Will. Spiritual Truth is significant because God is significant and worthy of being served.

How to Know Spiritual Truth
Though there are many ways in which people approach the Bible, we of this body believe the Bible, the whole Bible, and nothing but the Bible to be God's Word and sole authority in all matters of the Christian's faith (our beliefs), doctrine (our teachings), and practice (the way we live). Under-standing our responsibility to make known the divine message of the Bible, we present the following sessions as a statement of those basic truths taught in the Bible, which are common to the Christian faith, doctrine, and practice.

How to Use the FAQ Section

The FAQ of the Christian Faith has seven sections that progressively teach the gospel of Jesus the Christ. Each section contains the following:

- text that teaches various aspects of the gospel
- an illustration summarizing the teaching of the section
- step by step instructions how to draw the illustration
- questions pertaining to the section

Each section is called a session. Each session should take about twenty to thirty minutes to complete. Ideally, someone should try to read and complete one session every day in order to complete this FAQ workbook within one week.

After reading the text of a session the student should examine the corresponding illustration, draw out that day's illustration, and answer the questions. A student will need an 8.5" x 11" blank sheet of paper and pen or pencil. Drawing out each session is an important excise that should not be overlooked. Reading, seeing, creating, and reflecting are all important elements in comprehension.

Following each illustration is a series of questions pertaining to the session's text. The student should answer the questions pertaining to that day's session. The questions are designed to help in comprehending the main points of each session. The student will notice that the order of the questions directly corresponds to the session's text. For instance, question number one will deal with the first part of the text; question two will deal with the next part of the text; and so forth.

God has promised that His word will always do a work. His word is powerful and presently active. There are all kinds of reasons why people my want to understand the basics of Christianity. For those who desire to know God, He will reveal Himself clearly through His word.

F A Q

of the Christian Faith

As we begin, I have two questions: 1). "What is the passion or purpose of your life? (i.e. why are you here..? how do you wish to be remembered..?) and 2). On a scale of one through ten (ten being the best), how are you doing in living this out?" I would now like to share with you something someone once shared with me that helped me answer these two questions by explaining God's plan for Humanity.

Question #1:

Question #2:   1   2   3   4   5   6   7   8   9   10

Day 1: *Aspects of Sin*

In this chapter we consider three aspects of sin:
    1). What is sin?
    2). What is a sinner?
    3). Where did sin come from?

    Most people would not consider it a compliment if they were called a sinner. In fact, people often use this word in a demeaning or derogatory manner. The Bible does not use this word in this kind of harsh demoralizing fashion. The Bible uses the term "sinner" to describe one's spiritual nature. Being a sinner simply means that someone has a sin nature; and by acting upon this nature they sin. It should be understood that one's nature is not produced by one's actions.[2] It is actually quite the opposite; one's nature produces one's actions. A person's actions actually identifies the origin of one's nature. When you sin, it is because you have a nature or propensity to sin. Rest assured, as a sinner, you are not alone. The Bible actually states that every single human that has ever lived is a sinner.[3] As previously stated, being a sinner simply means that you have a nature or propensity to sin; but where did you get this sin nature?

    To answer this question, we need to go all the way back to the beginning of time. In the beginning there was a holy and just God. He has always been, and always will be, a holy and perfect God.[4] He created everything: the heavens and earth, the plants, all the animals, and He also created the first humans – Adam and Eve.[5] He formed Adam's body from the dust of the ground. Then God breathed the breath of life into Adam's nostrils and he became a living being.[6] God created Adam with both physical and spiritual life. Since God is the creator, His nature is the standard by which everything else is compared. At this time, all of God's creation, including human beings, possessed and reflected God's holy and perfect nature.[7]
In Genesis, the first book of the Bible, we also learn that God placed Adam in a special garden in a place called Eden.[8] This was a place where Adam could have a perfect ideal relationship with God through his worship and obedience. There were all kinds of fruit trees in this garden, including the tree of the knowledge of good and evil which

Day 1: *Aspects of Sin*

was in the middle of the garden. God instructed Adam, "You are free to eat from any tree in the garden; but you must not eat from the tree of the knowledge of good and evil, for when you eat of it you will surely die."[9] God provided for Adam's every need so Adam could reflect God's nature in his relationship with his Creator.[10]

God also created Eve with both a physical and spiritual life.[11] She received the same instructions about the forbidden fruit in the middle of the garden. A serpent (i.e. Satan) approached her and tried to convince her to eat the fruit from the tree of the knowledge of good and evil. The first four words the Devil said to humanity was, "Did God actually say..?" Satan, even to this very day, constantly tries to get people to doubt or question their understanding of God's word. Satan asked Eve, "Did God actually say, 'You shall not eat of any tree in the garden'?" Eve answered him, "We may eat fruit from the trees in the garden, but God did say, 'You must not eat fruit from the tree that is in the middle of the garden, and you must not touch it, or you will die.'"[12] Did you notice that Eve did not exactly understand or say what God had told Adam? This gave the serpent the foothold he needed in order to deceive and manipulate her.

Tragically, Satan was successful in deceiving Eve, convincing her that she misunderstood what God had said, so she ate the fruit from the tree of the knowledge of good and evil. After Eve ate the forbidden fruit she also gave some to her husband who was with her, and he also ate.[13] When this happened, for the very first time, sin entered the world through Adam's act of disobeying God's Word.[14] All of God's creation, not just Adam and Eve, was affected. God's creation no longer perfectly reflected God's nature and character. It was now tainted by what Adam had done. The Creator's desired relationship with Adam was altered due to his disobedience, or what the Bible calls sin. Sin is simply missing the mark. This is any action that does not perfectly reflect the nature of God.[15] Adam and Eve had become sinners (i.e. they had acquired a sin nature). Their actions have a direct effect on all of creation.

Day 1: *Aspects of Sin*

In summary, sin is any thought, word, or deed that does not reflect the character or nature of God. This occurs anytime someone does not obey God's word perfectly.[16] A sinner is a person who has the nature to sin; that is, they reflect the nature of Satan rather than the nature of God. The author or originator of sin is Satan. Lucifer was the most beautiful angelic created being. The dilemma for Lucifer was that He had pride. He rejected God and wanted humanity to worship him instead of God.[17] He relied on himself instead of trusting in God. This caused the most beautiful angel to fall from his lofty prestigious position.[18] We commonly know this angel by the name of Satan, the Devil, the Adversary, ruler of this world, etc. Have you ever had pride? Have you ever wanted the praise of men instead of having men praise God? Have you ever rejected God and relied on your abilities instead of trusting God? Of course you have! Because a sinner possesses the nature of Satan. As we will see in the next chapter, as a result of Adam's sin, every single person is a sinner.

The following diagram illustrates the summary of this chapter:

- The line drawn across the folded paper represents an eternal timeline. A holy and just God has no beginning and no end.

- The word "God" on the left side of the page represents the one true holy God of the Bible.

- The male stick figure on the right represents Adam.

- The female stick figure on the right represents Eve.

- The "P" above the stick figures represents their physical life.

- The "S" above the stick figures represents their spiritual life.

- The word "sin" represents the sin of Adam that affected all of creation.

Day 1: *Aspects of Sin*

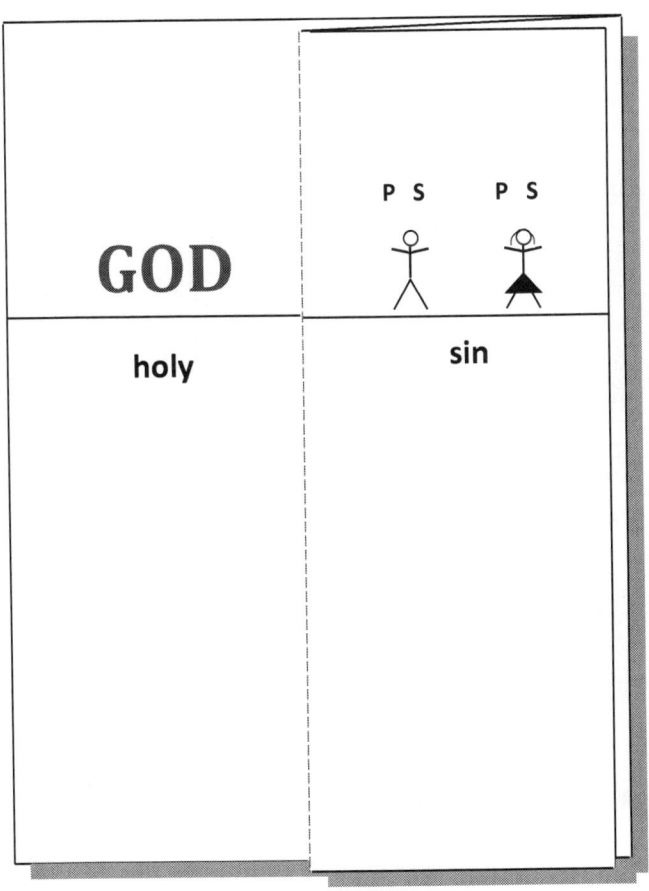

Day 1: *Aspects of Sin*

Drawing Session 1: *Aspects of Sin*

Fold the right side of a piece of paper (preferably 8½" by 11") in half over the left side (i.e. as seen in letter "A" below).

Fold just the back half of the paper in half again (i.e. letter "B" below).

The paper should now look like letter "C" below.

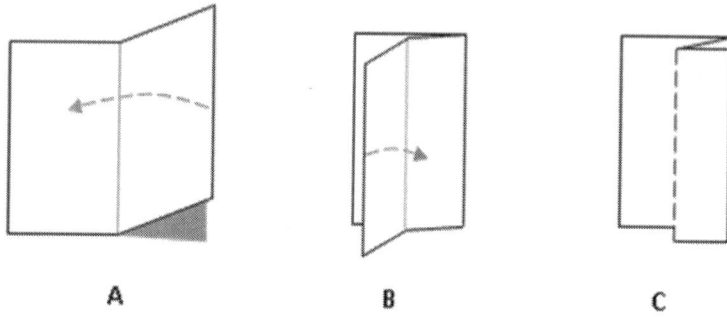

Draw a horizontal line about a third the way down across the folded piece of paper. Write "**GOD**" above line on left and "**holy**" under line.

Draw a man stick figure above line on the right with a "**P**" (i.e. for physical life) and an "**S**" (i.e. for spiritual life) above the stick figure.

Draw a woman stick figure next to the man with "**P**" and "**S**" above.

Write "**sin**" under the stick figure to represent their disobedience to God's word.

Day 1: *Aspects of Sin*

Questions for Session 1: *Aspects of Sin*

1.0   According to the Bible, how many people are sinners?

2.0   What is God's nature like?

3.1   What did God tell Adam that he was allowed to do?

3.2   What did God tell Adam that he was not allowed to do?

3.3   What did God tell Adam would happen if he did the very thing that God told him not to do?

3.4   Why did Eve eat the fruit from the tree of knowledge of good and evil?

3.5   Who gave the forbidden fruit to Adam?

4.0   What is sin?

Day 2: *Effects of Sin*

In this chapter we will explore three effects of sin:
1). What effect did Adam's sin have on the spiritual world?
2). What effect did Adam's sin have on the physical world?
3). What effect did Adam's sin personally have on you?

God had previously established the penalty for disobeying His word. The consequence of Adam's sin was death.[19] Since God is a holy and just God, He is always true to His word. God, being true to His word, immediately imposed the penalty of death. God always keeps His word – this is part of His nature![20]

There are two aspects of death, each corresponding to the two aspects of man – physical death and spiritual death.[21] Death simply means separation. In physical death, the soul is separated from the physical body. Without the soul, the body ceases to function.[22] In spiritual death, the soul is separated from God (i.e. the source of life). As God promised, when Adam and Eve ate the fruit from the tree of knowledge of good and evil, Adam and Eve immediately spiritually died. This means they became spiritually dead; that is, separated from God! It was just as though a huge bottomless pit had opened between God and mankind. God is on one side and mankind completely spiritually isolated from God on the other. Man became sinful and therefore became separated from their holy Creator.

When man brought sin into the world by disobeying God's Word, Adam and Eve acquired a sin nature. Their thoughts, words, and actions became a reflection of their new spiritual father, Satan, instead of a reflection of their Creator God.[23] In fact, mankind became a prisoner or enslaved to sin.[24] The only choice they now possessed was to sin. Their sin nature is what now dictated their actions. When they acquired a sin nature, as God had promised, mankind died spiritually. Adam and Eve became slaves to sin and were no longer able to fulfill their intended purpose; which was, to glorify God through obedience within a perfect ideal relationship with their Creator.

Day 2: *Effects of Sin*

After Adam and Eve had sinned against God, they were ejected from the garden in Eden.[25] Not only did they immediately spiritually die, they began to physically die as well. Since God gave Adam responsibility over all of creation, all of creation was affected by his sin. Things began to change. There was now pestilence, diseases, and eventually physical death.[26] Everything began to degenerate. This is evident to this day. Are things improving? Is the gene pool getting more pure or more diluted? Are we acquiring more new species or are we losing species? It is estimated (depending on which science camp you fall in) there are between 2000 up to 100,000 species going extinct every single year. The point is, when Adam and Eve sinned and sin entered all of creation, this not only had an immediate effect on their spiritual condition, but it altered all of the physical creation as well.

Adam and Eve lived what we might consider a 'normal' life. Though they were physically dying, they lived to be very old and had many children, who had many children, and so on. All the people from Adam and Eve to you and me have inherited some common human characteristics from Adam. We have ten fingers, ten toes, hair, two eyes, two ears, etc. Along with these characteristics, we also all inherited a human nature; the same type of nature as possessed by Adam. All of us were physically born into this world with a sin nature, which our "father" Adam acquired when he disobeyed God in the garden in Eden. This sin nature has been inherited and passed on from one generation to the next. You might say, "It is in our jeans" (ha ha, an intentional pun on genes).

Since we all have inherited and entered this world with the same sin nature as Adam and Eve, we also enter the world spiritually separated from God as a slave to sin (i.e. spiritually dead). We have an everlasting soul but it is spiritually dead; that is, separated from God. Not only are we spiritually dead, we are all physically dying. We are all in an environment that is self-destructive and degenerating. We have all inherited a sin nature, as well as other human characteristics, but we cannot inherit spiritual life through our parents. We must receive spiritual life from God. Up to this point, things may seem very grim and negative. Keep reading... it eventually gets mind-blowingly better.

Day 2: *Effects of Sin*

In Summary, the Bible says sin ultimately produces death (i.e. separation, destruction, degeneration, etc.). The following diagram illustrates the summary of this chapter:

- Putting an "**X**" through the "**S**" above each stick figure represents the spiritual death Adam and Eve immediately experienced when Adam disobeyed and sinned against God. This also represents the type of nature they now both possessed; that is, a sin nature.

- Opening up the folded piece of paper and drawing lines down each side, represents the spiritual separation that every human being experiences due to inheriting a sin nature from Adam.

- Writing "Physical Birth" on the top right side represents the only type of life that can be produced by humanity. We can only pass on physical life but we cannot give spiritual life.

- Drawing additional stick figures below the original two stick figures, represents the all the generations from Adam and Eve to you and me. Notice that all these generations are born with physical life, but none of them can be born with spiritual life. All the generations from Adam and Eve to you and me have been born spiritually separated from God.

Day 2: *Effects of Sin*

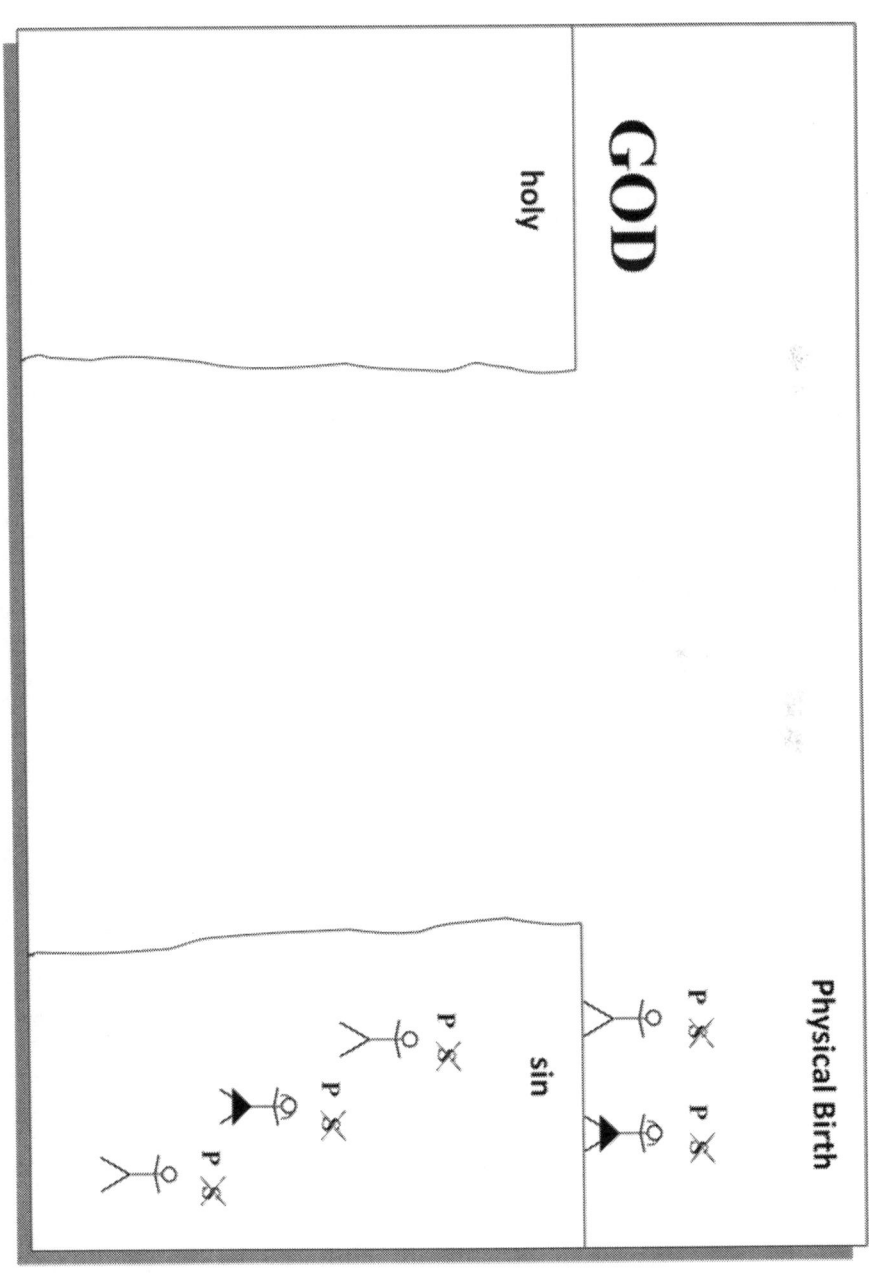

Day 2: *Effects of Sin*

Drawing Session 2: *Effects of Sin*

Write an "**X**" through the "**S**" above each stick figure to represent the spiritual death Adam and Eve immediately experienced when they disobeyed and sinned against God. This also represents the type of nature they now both possessed; that is, a sin nature.

Opening up the folded piece of paper and drawing lines down each side, represents the spiritual separation (i.e. spiritual death) that every human experiences due to inheriting a sin nature from Adam.

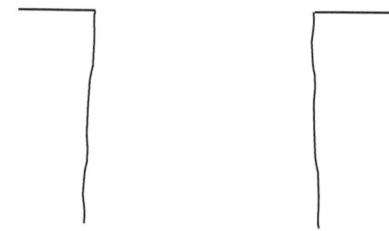

Write "**Physical Birth**" on the top right side to represent the only type of life that can be produced by humanity. We can only pass on physical life but we cannot give spiritual life.

Physical Birth

Drawing additional stick figures below the original two stick figures, represents all the generations from Adam and Eve to you and me. Notice that all these generations are born with physical life, but none of them can be physically born with spiritual life. All the generations from Adam and Eve to you and me have been physically born spiritually separated from God.

Day 2: *Effects of Sin*

Questions for Session 2: *Effects of Sin*

1.0 What immediately happened when Adam and Eve disobeyed God's word (i.e. sinned)?

2.1 What does it mean to die physically?

2.2 What does it mean to die spiritually?

3.0 After Adam sinned, what nature did Adam and Eve inherit?

4.0 What are some consequences due to Adam disobeying God's word (i.e. sinning)?

5.0 When parents have a sin nature, what kind of nature will their children inherit?

6.0 **True** or **False**. When an innocent little baby is physically born, they are born spiritually dead as a sinner; that is, spiritually separated from God.

Day 3: *Human Methods*

In this chapter we will explore:
1). How does humanity try to get to God?
2). What are four common examples of human efforts trying to obtain spiritual life?

    There are several ways that humanity tries to restore their broken relationship with God. People often try to get to God through their own efforts by building what we will call "human bridges." The sin nature naturally causes us to create and do things on our own instead of relying and trusting in God. We will even try to accomplish spirituality through our carnal ability which is motivated by our sin nature. It is a common misconception that if we try to do spiritual things then we will become spiritual. Or if we try to look and act spiritual then we will become spiritual. This makes perfect sense according to our sin nature, but it is not consistent with God's nature. To clarify this point, let's consider some common "bridges" people often attempt to build.

    One of the bridges people try to build is "Good Works." People often believe if they do things that appear to be God-like or good, then they will be accepted by God. People commonly believe that if they do more good things than bad, then God will reward the good and forget about or overlook the bad. Unfortunately, God is not impressed with our good works. In fact, the Bible says our good deeds are as impressive to God as a pile of filthy disgusting used dirty rags.[27] All goodness has its origin with God, not with sinful man. Our attempts of acting good fall far short of spanning the chasm of our spiritual separation from God. Good works cannot deliver us from spiritual death over to spiritual life.

    "Prayer" is another bridge people often rely on to spiritually reunite them to God. Many people believe that they must sincerely ask God to forgive their sins or say some kind of prayer for their relationship with God to be restored. It is almost if God were viewed as a genie in a magic bottle. If we ask God, then God will hop to and grant our request. Prayer is a way in which someone who has a restored relationship with God can communicate with their Creator;

Day 3: *Human Methods*

however, there is not any prayer that will restore a broken relationship, or bridge the gap, between mankind and God.

There are many people sitting in the pews of prominent, and not so prominent, churches that are trusting in church membership and/or attending "Church Gatherings" to bridge the gap between God and mankind. The Bible teaches that everyone who has had their relationship with God restored belong or are a part of the true church known as the ecclesia (i.e. called out ones). This is a spiritual group that God assembles, not a physical group that regularly has meetings. There is no group or regular assembly of people we can join that will restore our broken relationship with God. "Going to church" cannot reconcile man to God.

Although there are many bridges people attempt to build to try and reach God, for purposes of this illustration, the last bridge we will consider is the "Baptism" bridge. The word baptize is a transliterated word from the Koiné Greek language. The word simply means to be so immersed or saturated with something that you are identified with it. For instance, someone can be baptized in fear; meaning, they are so full of fear that if you look at them you would recognize that they are scared to death. Or someone could be baptized in love. We have all seen those couples that are oozing with love as they gaze into each other's eyes (Oh, yuck). Usually people reference baptism with being immersed or saturated with water. If one is relying on this baptism to bridge their relationship with God, they are simply all wet. Baptism with water can never restore one's relationship with God.

Though all these bridges fall far short in bridging the relational gap between mankind and God, it must be made perfectly clear that each of the so called bridges we discussed can have a very important place in our spiritual life. Spiritual actions flow out of spiritual people. But simply doing spiritual actions does not make someone spiritual. Humans put value on the outward actions, but God looks on the heart.[28] The dilemma for mankind is the heart. We need God to give us a new heart (i.e. new nature), and then spiritual actions will flow

Day 3: *Human Methods*

out of that new nature. No bridge humanity tries to build has the ability to give spiritual life! It is only after someone has been given spiritual life that spiritual actions can fulfill their designed purpose.

In summary, it is human nature to try and do things to reconcile the broken relationship between God and mankind. There are all kinds of religions and spiritual activities that mankind practices in order to try to become more spiritual. No action mankind does can bridge the relational gap between man and God.

The following diagram illustrates the summary of this chapter:

- The first platform or "bridge" is "Good Works." As can be seen in the illustration, the bridge of good works falls far short of bridging the gap between mankind and God.

- The next bridge is "Prayer." Simply asking, begging, or talking to God can never restore one's broken spiritual relationship to God. Individuals need a new heart. Putting one's hope in prayer is not the way to gain a new heart or nature.

- The next bridge is "Church Gatherings." Many well intended people put an emphasis on going to an event they call "church" or joining an exclusive "membership." From Genesis through Revelation, the Bible records man's failed attempts to please or gain access to God through various organized events.

- Though there are many spiritual things people try to do to please God in order to restore their broken relationship, for our purposes the last bridge is "Baptism." Again, many well intended people have trusted that they have a healthy relationship with God because they were immersed or saturated with water. There is no amount of water that can restore the broken spiritual relationship between humanity and God.

Day 3: *Human Methods*

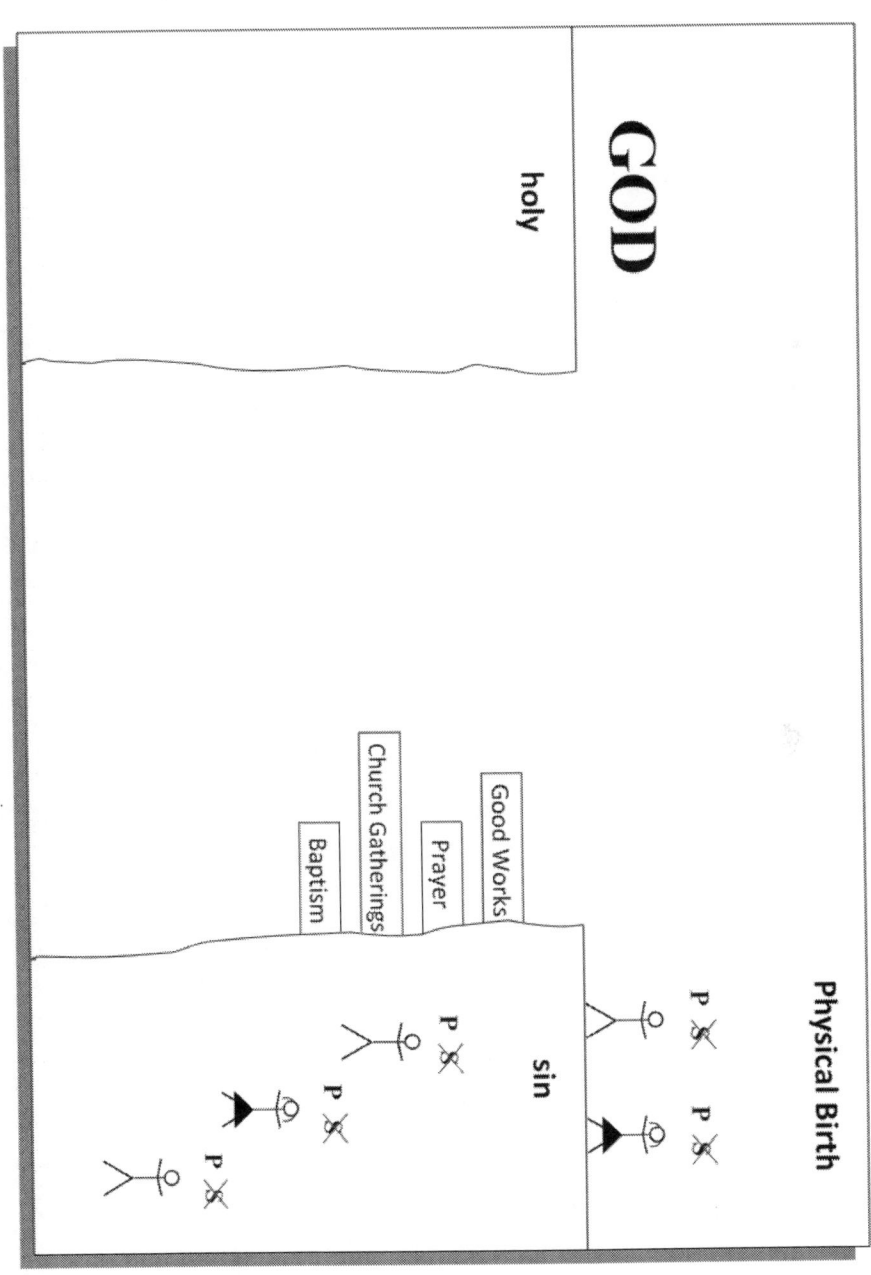

Day 3: *Human Methods*

Drawing Session 3: *Human Methods*

Draw the "Good Works" bridge and write "**Good Works**" inside of it

Good Works

Prayer

Church Gatherings

Baptism

Draw the "Prayer" bridge and write "**Prayer**" inside of it

Draw the "Church Gatherings" bridge and write "**Church Gatherings**" inside of it

Draw the "baptism" bridge and write "**Baptism**" inside of it

Day 3: *Human Methods*

Questions for Session 3: *Human Methods*

1.0 **True** or **False**. If someone desires to be spiritual then they must look and act spiritual.

2.0 Compared to the goodness of God, what does the bible say our good works (i.e. good deeds) are like?

3.0 **True** or **False**. In order for people to restore their broken relationship with God, they must earnestly pray for God to forgive them of their sins.

4.0 What is the true church here on earth?

5.0 What does the word "baptize" mean?

6.0 **True** or **False**. There is no spiritual value in doing spiritual things.

Day 4: *Trusting False gods*

In this chapter we will explore:
1). Does God exist?
2). What is a false god?
3). What are the consequences of trusting in a false god?

    Before someone could even try to reconcile their spiritual relationship with God, one must acknowledge and understand the reality or existence of God. The Bible never tries to prove God's existence. The Bible simply states the fact, "In the beginning God created…" The Bible states that God has clearly shown His eternal power and divine nature through creation; but, mankind will often not honor Him as God or even acknowledge Him. People all too often turn their hearts away from God instead of pursuing a relationship with Him. In conclusion of this thought, the Bible says men are without any excuses because they should have known better, even if for no other reason, because creation reveals the evidence of God.[29]

    A friend recently told me an interesting story: There were two close friends that took very different paths in their youth. One became a devout believer in God, and the other an atheist. The atheist would claim that there is no evidence of God while the believer proclaimed that, at the very least, creation demonstrates the existence of God. The atheist became a devoted scientist who specialized in astronomy and said all of creation appeared by chance happenings. For his birthday, the believer had one of his engineering friends design and build a very precise working scale model of our solar system. All the planets were rotating at just the right speeds as they orbited the sun in their exact elliptical paths and velocities. The atheist was delighted with his gift. As he explored this replica of the universe, he was amazed at the accuracy and precision of the scale model. In complete astonishment the atheist asked, "Who was the engineer who designed and created this beautiful scale model. His believing friend simply replied, "No one, it just appeared by chance over billions of years. I simply discovered it and gave it to you." God is a revealing Creator who can be seen and known. He desires to have a personal relationship with His creation.

Day 4: *Trusting False gods*

As long as we are separated from God, our human devices and attempts to reach Him will be to no avail. Realizing that there is a God is perhaps the first step in pursuing reconciliation. It is only after someone comes to the realization that a personal revealing Creator actually exists, that they can pursue getting to know Him. Unfortunately, even after this realization, people will often be led astray by creating faulty systems or religions. These faulty systems or religions becomes their false faith in a false god. This is the god in which they are trusting. In fact, everyone has faith in something whether they believe in God or not. Even the atheist has faith that there is no true faith. Our present culture is plagued with relativism. The only absolute truth that the relative thinker adopts is that there is absolutely no such thing as absolute truth. And they are absolutely sure that there is no absolute truth. Since there is only one true God, then there is only one true faith. Everyone has a god. Whatever people are truly trusting or believing in becomes their god.

The tragedy is that when one's physical life on this earth comes to an end, and if they are still separated from God (i.e. spiritually dead) because of having trusted in erroneous ways of restoring their relationship with God, they will remain in that state forever. They will be separated from God forever in a place often referred to as hell (i.e. hades, the second death, lake of fire, etc.). The Bible calls this the second death because it is not the first death. The first death is the physical death, whereas the second death references spiritual death. And do you know how the Bible describes spiritual death? The second death is the complete separation from God in total darkness and isolation, under perpetual judgment and torment, without hope, forever and ever and ever![30] It is impossible for anyone to even begin to imagine how utterly horrible it is to be completely and permanently separated from God. Nor can words describe the misery that will be experienced by mind, soul, and body. Imagine spending forever in such a place apart from God. And the saddest reality is that this is totally unnecessary!

Day 4: *Trusting False gods*

It is not God's desire that any person should be separated from Him in such a place.[31] It is His desire that every person would cross the chasm of separation and be united with Him in a perfect restored eternal relationship. God desires that every person should have spiritual life and spend eternity in a perfect relationship with Him. Because of His immeasurable love for us, His great mercy and amazing grace, God has provided a way for us to cross the great chasm separating mankind from God. God was under no obligation to do this. It is only out of His loving nature that God has provided a way for our relationship to be perfectly restored.[32]

In summary, there is only one true God and therefore only one absolute truth and only one true faith. God's existence is evident through creation. No one has any excuses for denying the existence of God. No one has any excuse for not pursuing a relationship with their Creator. The Bible says, "The fool says in his heart, 'There is no God.' They are corrupt, they do abominable deeds, there is none who does good."[33] In actuality, whether they realize it or not, whatever people are trusting in is their god. This could be science, one's own intellect, materialism, false religions, the bridges in our diagram, etc. There are eternal consequences in having faith in anything or anyone other than the one true God. If someone experiences the first death without having true faith in the one true God, they will experience the second death (i.e. spiritual death).

The following diagram illustrates the summary of this chapter:

- All the arrows going down from the "bridges" represent people having faith in false gods when they die.

- Writing the word "Hell" at the end of these arrows represents the second death (i.e. spiritual death).

Day 4: *Trusting False gods*

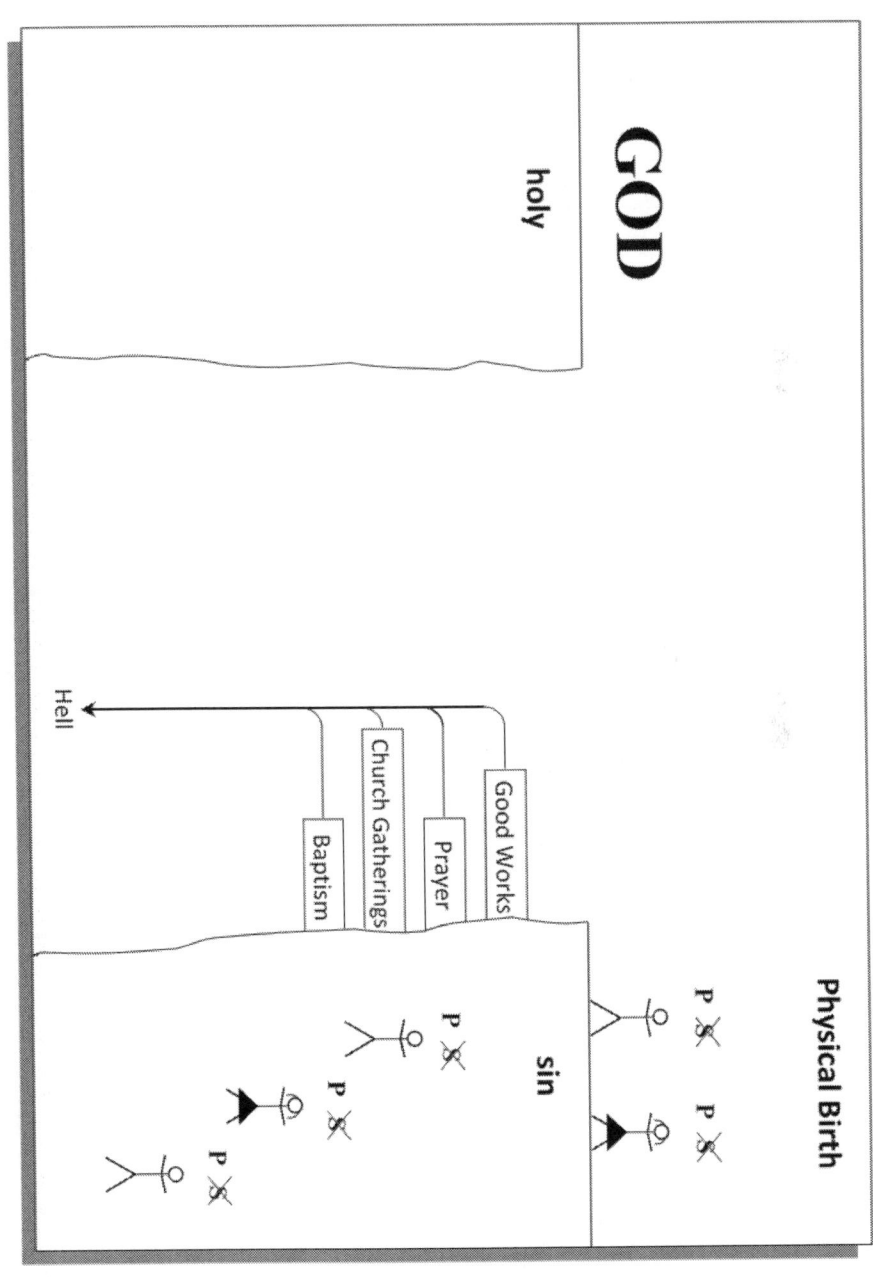

Day 4: *Trusting False gods*

Drawing Session 4: *Trusting False gods*

Draw the arrows downward from the human bridges.

Write the word "**Hell**" at the bottom of the arrow. This word represents the second death and the eternal consequences in having faith in anything or anyone other than the one true God.

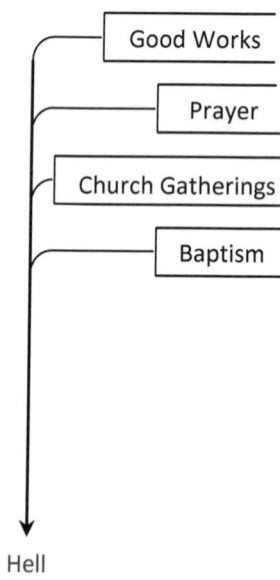

Day 4: *Trusting False gods*

Questions for Session 4: *Trusting False gods*

1.0 What is at least one thing that clearly shows God's invisible attributes; namely, his eternal power and divine nature?

2.0 **True** or **False**. Everyone believes in a god.

3.0 **True** or **False**. Since there is only one true God, there is only one absolute truth and only one true faith.

4.0 Describe the first death and the second death.

5.0 What is God's desire concerning His relationship with mankind?

6.0 According to the Bible, what does the fool say in his heart and how is a fool described?

Day 5: *The Way to God*

In this chapter we will explore:
1). Who is the way, the truth, and the life?
2). What has Jesus done in order to restore mankind to God?
3). Why would a good man like Jesus die for a sinner like me?

Do you know the way to God? Jesus the Christ said, "I am the way, and the truth, and the life. No one comes to the Father except through me."[34] Jesus did not say that good works, prayer, church gatherings, baptism, or anything else is the way. He said: "I am *the way*." God the Son was sent by God the Father into this world to become The Bridge between mankind and God. He is the only way by which we may cross the spiritual chasm created by sin. Sin produces spiritual death but God's love through Jesus the Christ produces spiritual life. "For God so loved the world, that he gave his only Son, that whoever believes in him should not perish but have eternal life."[35] By placing faith in Jesus as the only true way, one is placing faith in the one true God.

Not only did Jesus say He is the only way, Jesus also stated that there are no exceptions. He said that *no one* can come to God except through Him. There are no exceptions! We may not like it. We may not think this is fair, but this is the reality. Accepting or trusting in anything but Jesus will lead to the second death. This is the truth. Jesus said He is the way and *the truth*. There is only one Jesus and there is only one truth. Knowing the truth will set a person free.[36] The truth will free the individual who is enslaved by sin through their sin nature. Jesus the Christ is the way and the truth.

Jesus also said He is *the life*. Trusting in Him alone will give spiritual life. Through faith in Christ, an individual will cross over from spiritual death to spiritual life. And Jesus does not give just any kind of life; he gives eternal life. The idea behind eternal life is not just simply the longevity of life, but the quality of life.[37] The spiritual life obtained through faith in Jesus is like no other. Christ gives an abundant life of the highest quality.[38] It is infinite, beyond description, provides peace that is surpasses all understanding; it is eternal life. Jesus is the way, the truth, and the life.

Day 5: *The Way to God*

What did Jesus Christ actually do to become this bridge? By shedding His blood and dying upon the cross, being buried in the grave, and resurrected the third day according to the scriptures, Jesus became the life-giving savior for mankind.[39] God the Son (i.e. Jesus the Christ) is always in perfect harmonious fellowship with God the Father.[40] His entire existence is purposed to obey the Father in order to reveal the Father for the Father's glory. Glorifying God the Father is the core essence of Jesus' Personhood.[41] Though the physical agony of enduring an execution by means of crucifixion was horrific, there was something far worse Jesus endured. He pleaded with the Father, if it were at all possible (and with God all things are possible) for the Father to not ask Him to go to the cross.[42] Again, Jesus was not afraid of the physical pain (though I am sure he wasn't looking forward to it). He could not bear to be separated from His Father. Anything but that! None the less, Jesus conceded His own will to be obedient to the will of the Father. He obediently went to the cross and took on the sin of the world.[43] He experienced the full wrath of God. He experienced the full brunt of the second death multiplied by the number of humans that will ever live. Wow!

I am constantly amazed that the Father would have Jesus the Christ die for me. I can see if someone were to take a bullet for a good or important man, but to give your life for a sinner who did not even know or acknowledge God? Not only am I completely wretched, but Jesus is as perfect as God is perfect.[44] Jesus the Christ is God Himself who became flesh being born in the likeness of man.[45] He was born of a virgin.[46] He did not have a sin nature; but rather, He has the nature of His heavenly Father (i.e. God). The Bible describes God's perfection as righteous. Every sinner is unrighteous. Christ is righteous (i.e. without sin) and therefore did not deserve to die, but He died in our place (i.e. the unrighteous). "For Christ also suffered once for sins, the righteous for the unrighteous, that he might bring us to God."[47] "For one will scarcely die for a righteous person— though perhaps for a good person one would dare even to die— but God shows his love for us in that while we were still sinners, Christ died for us."[48]

Day 5: *The Way to God*

In summary, much like Adam's act of disobedience had a negative spiritual effect, Jesus' act of obedience has a positive spiritual effect. He is the way, the truth, and the life. No one comes to God the Father apart from Him.

The following diagram illustrates the summary of this chapter:

- The cross with "Jesus the Christ" written in the middle represents that Jesus is the way, the truth, and the life. He is The Bridge that God the Father has provided so mankind can cross over from spiritual death to spiritual life.

- John 14:6. "Jesus said to him, 'I am the way, and the truth, and the life. No one comes to the Father except through me.'"

- John 3:16. "For God so loved the world, that he gave his only Son, that whoever believes in him should not perish but have eternal life."

- 1 Peter 3:18a. "For Christ also suffered once for sins, the righteous for the unrighteous, that he might bring us to God…"

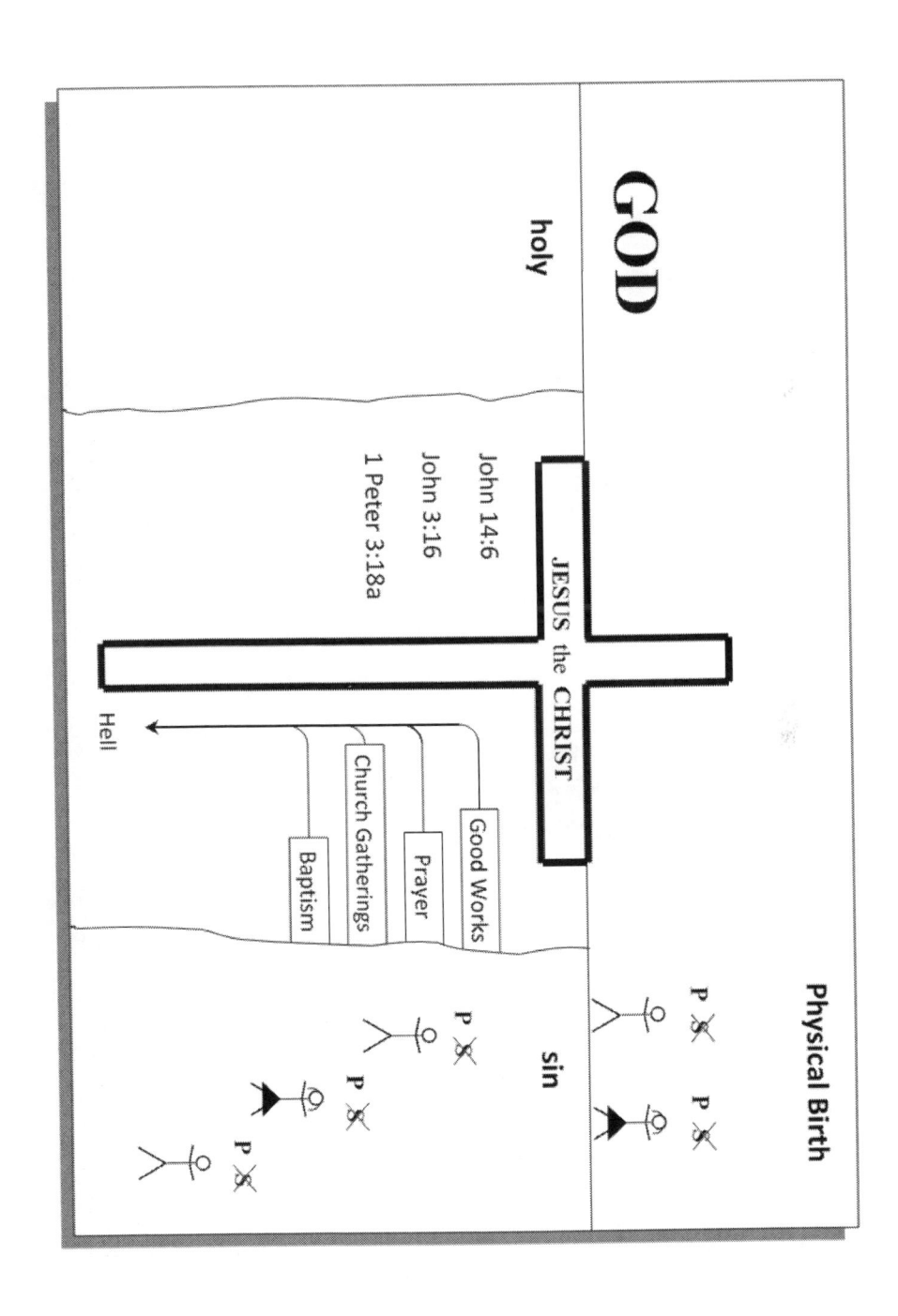

Day 5: *The Way to God*

GOD

holy

JESUS the CHRIST

John 14:6
John 3:16
1 Peter 3:18a

Baptism
Church Gatherings
Prayer
Good Works

Hell

sin

Physical Birth

Day 5: *The Way to God*

Drawing Session 5: *The Way to God*

Write "**John 14:6**" on the left side of the chasm.

Write "**John 3:16**" under "John 14:6"

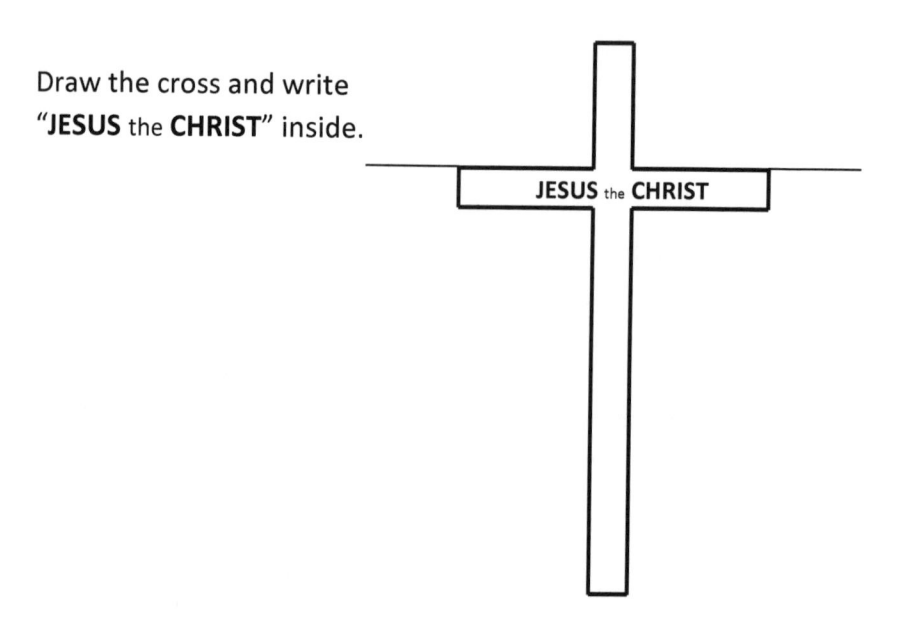

Draw the cross and write "**JESUS** the **CHRIST**" inside.

JESUS the CHRIST

Write "**1 Peter 3:18a**" under "John 3:16"

Session 5: *The Way to God*

Questions for Session 5: *The Way to God*

1.0 What did Jesus say concerning the way to God, the truth about God, and true spiritual life?

2.1 What did Jesus actually do in order to become the bridge so that we can cross over from spiritual death to spiritual life?

2.2 Why would Jesus do this?

3.0 Look up in the Bible and write out the verse John 14:6.

4.0 Look up in the Bible and write out the verse John 3:16.

5.0 Look up in the Bible and write out the verse 1 Peter 3:18.

Day 6: *Being Born Again*

In this chapter we will explore:
1). What does it mean to be born again?
2). How does someone become a child of God?
3). What is the Tri-unity of God?

When we come to God by having faith in Jesus Christ, we pass from spiritual death to spiritual life. God gives us spiritual life.[49] We now have the highest quality of life (i.e. eternal life) that can never be taken away. One of the passages in the Bible that speaks of this life is 1 John 5:11 and 12, "And this is the testimony, that God gave us eternal life, and this life is in his Son. Whoever has the Son has life; whoever does not have the Son of God does not have life."

In John 3:1-10, the Bible tells us about a man named Nicodemous who came to Jesus to make inquiries of Him. Jesus explained to Nicodemous how he could cross the gulf of separation between him and God. Jesus said, "no one can enter the kingdom of God unless he is born again." Being born again is referencing a second birth. Nicodemous said to Jesus, "How can a man be born when he is old? Can he enter a second time into his mother's womb and be born?" Nicodemous understood the first birth is a physical birth but he was confused because he did not understand that the second birth Jesus was talking about is a spiritual birth. Everyone is born physically alive but spiritually dead. Our physical parents give physical birth but we need our spiritual parent (i.e. God) to give us spiritual birth. The Bible says that when we are united with Christ through faith, we become a new creation. Just like with any birth, when someone is spiritually born they are a born a new little spiritual baby.

There was a man named John the Baptist that came to prepare people for the coming of Jesus.[50] He baptized people in water as he proclaimed, "Repent, for the kingdom of heaven is at hand."[51] Repentance is to have a changed mind. We need to have a new heart which will give us a changed mind.[52] The idea is we need to be spiritually born a new person.[53] John the Baptist said he was baptizing with water, but Jesus was coming and would baptize people

Day 6: *Being Born Again*

with the Holy Spirit.[54] Jesus totally immerses or saturates people with the Holy Spirit so that they are identified with the Holy Spirit. At the moment someone believes (i.e. has faith, trusts, crosses over The Bridge, etc.) they are born again, or become regenerate. Upon regeneration, at that very moment, is when Jesus baptizes them with the Holy Spirit.

Who is the Holy Spirit? Just like the Father is God, and Jesus is God, so the Holy Spirit is God. Christ did not teach there are three Gods; by no means, He clearly taught there is only ONE GOD.[55] But Jesus clearly revealed that the one true God is God the Father; God the Son; and God the Holy Spirit; three Persons eternally coexisting in the Godhead, yet only one true God. Each Person is the exact same in substance, yet distinct in subsistence. This teaching is often known as the Trinity.[56] This is a difficult concept that can only be accepted and truly understood through faith by those that are born again (i.e. regenerate). Jesus gave His followers a command that they are to physically do which creates a symbolic picture of the tri-unity of God (i.e. trinity).

One of the great missions, or things Jesus was to accomplish, was to reveal God's name. At the end of Jesus' incarnate ministry, He said to His Father that He had accomplished all that the Father had sent Him to do. He said that He had perfectly revealed God's name.[57] The idea of revealing a name is to reveal the very essence or complete identity of a person. After Jesus was resurrected from the dead, right before He ascended up into heaven, He commanded His followers to go and help others know and follow His teachings (a follower of Jesus' teachings is called a disciple).[58] And one of the things He commanded His disciples to do was to go and make other disciples. They were to symbolically water baptize them into God's name. The command is to immerse them into the Father, and immerse them into the Son, and immerse them into the Holy Spirit.[59] Three dips yet only one baptism into the name of God. The symbolic Christian water baptism is a picture of a disciple being saturated and identified with the one true God; namely, God the Father, God the Son, and God the Holy Spirit. There are three dips yet only one

Day 6: *Being Born Again*

baptism, just like there are three Persons of the Godhead yet only one true God.

When we are born again, we become what the Bible calls a child of God. This new spiritual relationship is described in John 1:12-13, "But to all who did receive him, who believed in his name, he gave the right to become children of God, who were born, not of blood nor of the will of the flesh nor of the will of man, but of God." To be born again, to become a child of God, someone must receive Jesus and believe in His name. Again, when someone has faith (i.e. trusts, believes, etc.) in Jesus they receive Him. To believe in His name is to believe in the very essence, the true complete identity, of His very being.

What a great gift God has given us – to be part of His family. Through Jesus the Christ, we are adopted by God as His child and experience all the benefits of being a child of the Creator of the universe. Equally amazing is the fact that this newfound relationship with God is not something that will eventually happen. It is a now thing! We are born again and given eternal life at the very moment we believe and receive Christ through faith. We are a new creation and receive a new nature; the nature of our heavenly Father. Though a child of God still has their old sin nature, lives are changed the moment people come to God through Christ as they receive God's nature.[60] Is it any wonder life takes on a new wonderful meaning? Is it any wonder we want to get to know God better through the Bible or share the "Good News" of Jesus Christ with others?

The following diagram illustrates the summary of this chapter:

- the "Spiritual Birth" at the top left

- the people who crossed over The Bridge (i.e. who were born again) are spiritually alive (i.e. no "X" through the "S")

- the "Born Again (John 3:1-10)" above the line showing people crossing over the bridge

- and the additional verses "1 John 5:11-12 and John 1:12-13.

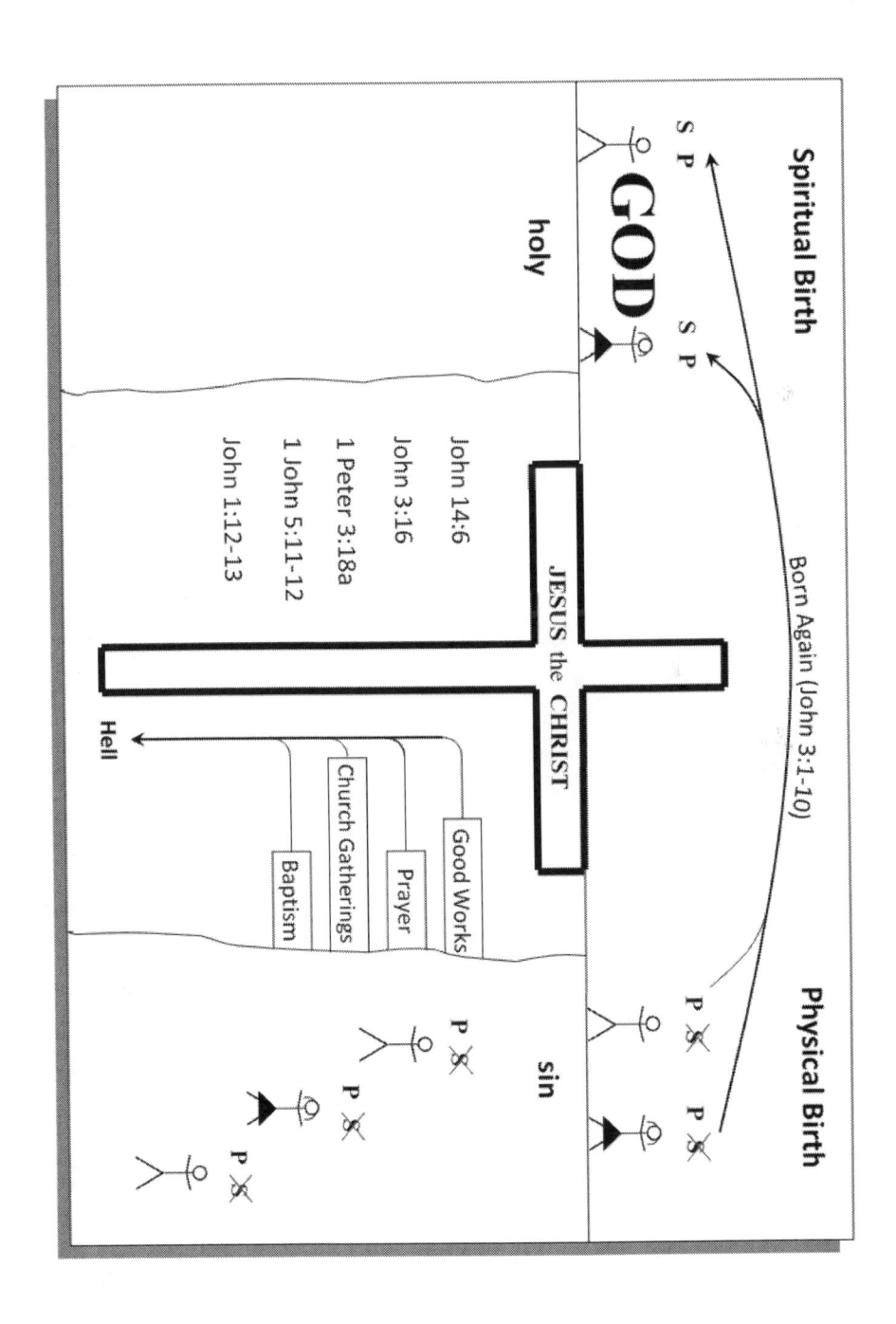

Day 6: *Being Born Again*

Spiritual Birth

GOD

holy

Born Again (John 3:1-10)

John 14:6
John 3:16
1 Peter 3:18a
1 John 5:11-12
John 1:12-13

JESUS the CHRIST

Good Works
Prayer
Church Gatherings
Baptism

Hell ←

sin

Physical Birth

Day 6: *Being Born Again*

Drawing Session 6: *Being Born Again*

Draw the two new stick figures on the other side of the chasm, one on each side next to God. Write an "**S**" for spiritual life and a "**P**" for physical life above each stick figure.

Draw an arrow from each stick figure on the "Physical Birth" side over to the "Spiritual Birth" side.

Write "**Spiritual Birth**" in the upper left-hand corner.

Write "**1 John 5:11-12**" under "1 Peter 3:18a."

Write "**Born Again (John 3:1-10)**" on top of the line connecting the stick figures.

Write "**John 1:12-13**" under "1 John 5:11-12."

Day 6: *Being Born Again*

Questions for Session 6: *Being Born Again*

1.1 According to 1 John 5:11-12, if someone has the Son (i.e. Jesus the Christ) what else do they have?

1.2 According to 1 John 5:11-12, if someone does not have the Son of God (i.e. Jesus the Christ) what else do they not have?

2.0 **What happens at the very moment when someone becomes a child of God** (i.e. believes in Jesus, receives Jesus, has faith or trusts in Jesus, accepts Jesus, crosses over The Bridge, becomes regenerate, born again, saved, etc.)**?**

3.1 The very essence or name of God is Trinitarian. God is _____ Persons yet only _____ true God.

3.2 Who are the three Persons of the one true God?

4.0 **True** or **False**. When someone becomes born again they become a new creation with the nature of their Heavenly Father; therefore, they will never sin anymore and life will be easy and they will be happy all the time.

Day 7: *God's Speed*

Eternal life is a gift! The Bible says, "For by grace you have been saved through faith. And this is not your own doing; it is the gift of God, not a result of works, so that no one may boast."[61] Receiving eternal life is not based on what we do, but rather on what God has done. God the Father has sent His Son. God the Son has sacrificially died on the cross and raised the third day. God the Holy Spirit gives us new birth through faith in Jesus the Christ.

The gift of eternal life is something no one deserves and which no one can repay. There is nothing anyone can do to merit God's grace – it is a gift! Grace is God's unmerited favor given to man. It is a gift given through faith. Only those who have received the gift of eternal life through faith in Christ can serve God through good works. When we are given this new life, we have a relationship with the Father and can actually talk with Him (i.e. prayer). We are part of His family (i.e. His church). We are spiritually baptized into the one true God.

When we receive the gift of eternal life we are saved – saved from the deserved wrath of God. "For all have sinned"[62] and deserve, or have earned, eternal death.[63] "But God shows his love for us in that while we were still sinners, Christ died for us."[64] Someone has to pay the due penalty of sin to a just and holy God. We have one of two choices: either we can receive the penalty for our sin (this yields eternal death and damnation) or we can allow Christ to receive the penalty for our personal sin (this yields eternal life). The Bible says every knee will bow and tongue confess Jesus is Lord.[65] You can either do this now through faith and receive eternal life *or* you will do this after you physically die and experience the second death. We are all at one spiritual place or another as we travel through this temporal journey we call life. As I have said, I am just one beggar telling another beggar where I found bread. If you can help find some more bread, I would be appreciative. If there is anything I could do to help you on your spiritual journey, I would be willing and honored. May we all have God's speed as we travel on this journey from the temporal to the eternal!

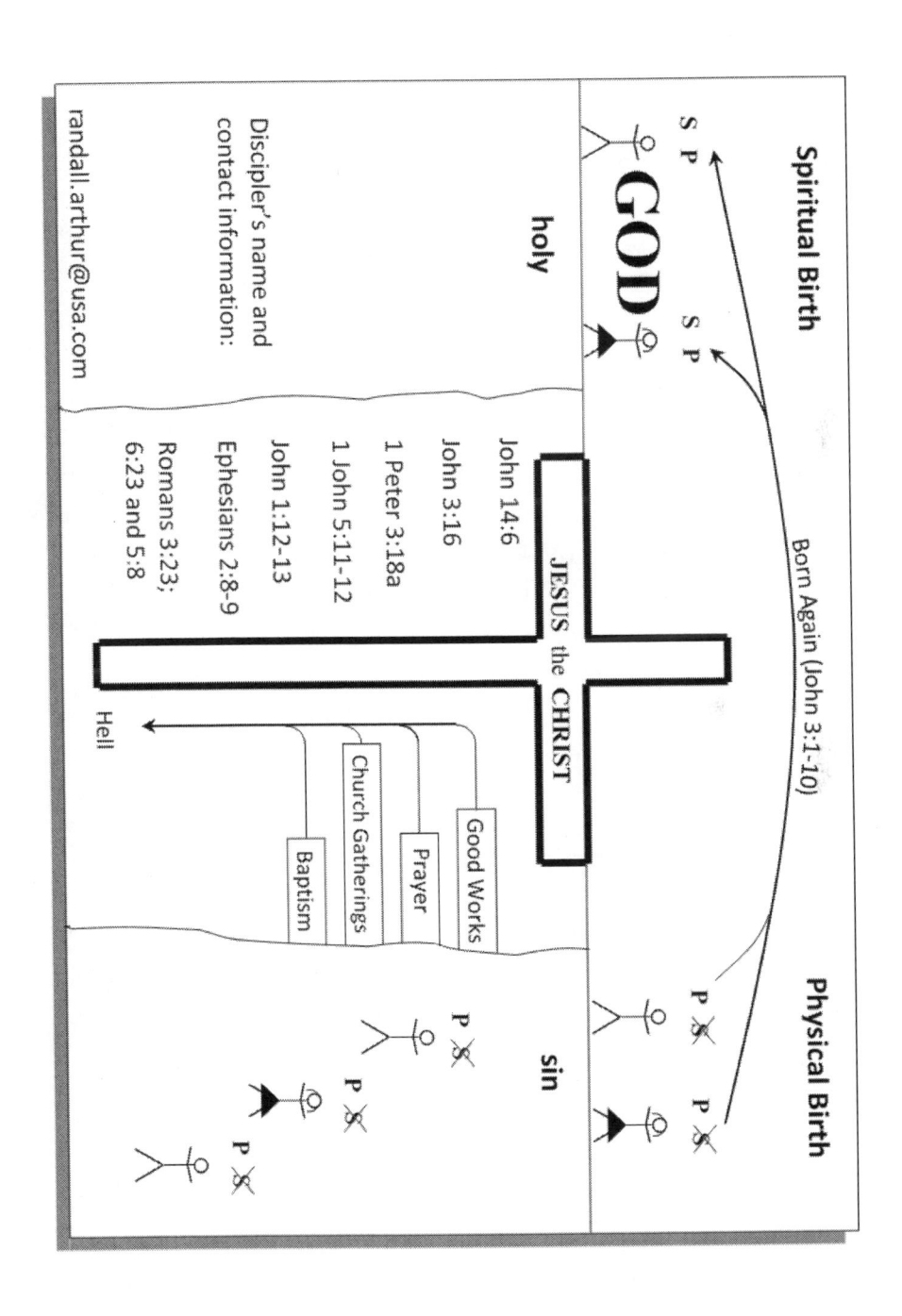

Day 7: *God's Speed*

Spiritual Birth

GOD

holy

Born Again (John 3:1-10)

JESUS the CHRIST

- John 14:6
- John 3:16
- 1 Peter 3:18a
- 1 John 5:11-12
- John 1:12-13
- Ephesians 2:8-9
- Romans 3:23; 6:23 and 5:8

Good Works
Prayer
Church Gatherings
Baptism

Hell

sin

Physical Birth

Discipler's name and contact information:

randall.arthur@usa.com

Day 7: *God's Speed*

So what's next? If you are a child of God, then the simplest answer to that question is to follow Jesus. But what exactly does it mean to follow Jesus? Jesus said that just as the Father has sent Him into the world, He is now sending us. The Father sent Jesus to glorify the Father by making Him known. The way to know the Father is by knowing Jesus. So how do you get to know Jesus? The only way to know Jesus is through the Holy Spirit revealing Him to us through the truth of the Scriptures. Here is a summary on how this all works:

- The purpose of our life is to glorify God. The way we glorify God is getting to know Him (i.e. having a restored relationship with Him) and helping others get to know Him.
- The only way to know Jesus is by having the Holy Spirit reveal Him to us through the truth of the Scripture.
- The only way to know the Father is by knowing Jesus.
- As the Father is made known, God is glorified.
- As we help people get to know God through the truth of the Scriptures, God is made known and therefore glorified.

So the next step is to learn how to properly interact, study, and interpret the Bible so you can get to know and glorify God. We have designed a discipleship curriculum to help in this process. If you would like more information on these materials, please do not hesitate to contact us.

We are all at one spiritual place or another as we travel through this temporal journey we call life. As I have said, I am just one beggar telling another beggar where I found bread. If you can help me find some more bread, I would be appreciative. If there is anything I could do to help you on your journey, I would be willing and honored: randall.arthur@usa.com. God's speed on your spiritual journey!

Scripture Endnotes

1. John 14:21
2. Matthew 7:15-20 with James 3:11-12
3. Romans 3:23 with 5:12, 18-19
4. Leviticus 11:44-45 with Hebrews 13:8 and Revelation 1:8
5. Genesis 1
6. Genesis 2:7
7. Genesis 1:27
8. Genesis 2:8
9. Genesis 2:16-17
10. Genesis 1:29-30; 2:10-11 with 2:15
11. Genesis 2:20-22
12. Genesis 3:2-3
13. Genesis 3:6-7
14. Romans 5:12
15. Romans 8:3-17
16. Romans 14:23
17. Isaiah 14:12-15
18. Luke 10:18
19. Romans 5:12 with Romans 6:23
20. Titus 1:2
21. Matthew 10:28
22. James 2:26
23. Romans 6:19 with Genesis 6:5
24. John 8:34 with Romans 6:19
25. Genesis 3:23-24
26. Genesis 3:17-18 with Romans 5:17
27. Isaiah 64:6
28. 1 Samuel 16:7
29. Romans 1:18-25
30. John 3:36 with Revelation 20:10, 14-15
31. 1 Timothy 2:3-4
32. 1 John 4:8-10
33. Psalm 14:1, 53:1

Scripture Endnotes

34. John 14:6
35. John 3:16
36. John 8:32
37. John 17:3
38. John 10:10
39. 1 Corinthians 15:2-4
40. John 10:31
41. Philippians 2:11
42. Luke 18:27
43. Philippians 2:8
44. Hebrews 4:15
45. John 1:1, 14
46. Luke 1:27, 34
47. 1 Peter 3:18a
48. Romans 5:7-8
49. Romans 4:17
50. John 1:6-7
51. Matthew 4:17
52. Ezekiel 36:26-27
53. 2 Corinthians 5:17
54. Luke 3:16
55. Deuteronomy 6:4
56. Matthew 3:16-17
57. John 17:4-6
58. Matthew 28:16-20
59. Matthew 28:19
60. Romans 7:13-20
61. Ephesians 2:8-9
62. Romans 3:23
63. Romans 6:23
64. Romans 5:8
65. Philippians 2:10-11

Session 1: *The Bible*

> **The Bible:** The sixty-six canonized books of the Old and New Testaments, as originally given, are the verbally breathed out by God (i.e. inspired), plenary, infallible, inerrant, complete and sufficient perspicuous sole Word of God in this present Church age. The Bible, the whole Bible, and nothing but the Bible is a Christian's sole authority in all matters of faith, doctrine, and practice (2 Timothy 3:16-17; 2 Peter 1:20-21). "When Scripture speaks God speaks, when Scripture is not speaking God is not speaking."

1.0 **Write the full name of the sixty-six books as they are commonly listed in the Bible and then write the abbreviation for each book in parenthesis next to its name** (the first one has been done for you).

1. Genesis	23.	45.
2.	24.	46.
3.	25.	47.
4.	26.	48.
5.	27.	49.
6.	28.	50.
7.	29.	51.
8.	30.	52.
9.	31.	53.
10.	32.	54.
11.	33.	55.
12.	34.	56.
13.	35.	57.
14.	36.	58.
15.	37.	59.
16.	38.	60.
17.	39.	61.
18.	40.	62.
19.	41.	63.
20.	42.	64.
21.	43.	65.
22.	44.	66.

Session 1: *The Bible*

2.1 How many "books" are there in the O. T. (i.e. Old Testament)?

2.2 How many books in the N. T. (i.e. New Testament)?

3.0 Look up the following in Webster's Dictionary and write a definition for each:

    a. Canon(ized) –

    b. Plenary –

    c. Infallible –

    d. Inerrant –

    e. Perspicuous –

4.0 According to 2 Timothy 3:16-17, how much of Scripture is "breathed out by God?" How much of Scripture is useful?

5.0 According to 2 Timothy 3:16-17, what is Scripture profitable for?

6.0 According to 2 Timothy 3:16-17, what does a "man of God" need in order to be complete and equipped for every good work?

Session 1: *The Bible*

Brief History of the Bible

When God guided men to write His Word, they wrote in their own language. The Old Testament was written mostly in Hebrew (with a few passages being written in Aramaic) while the New Testament was written in Greek. Since then, the Bible has been translated and copied into several different languages. In fact, portions of the Bible have been translated in over 2,000 different languages.

Because these books of the Bible were written hundreds (and in some cases thousands) of years before the first printing press, copies were handmade. Great precautions were made to keep each copy accurate, yet some very slight variations occurred between these copies. In 1516 A.D. the first Greek New Testament was printed on a press. The first English version of the Bible was printed in 1611.

The Bible we use today is derived from a thorough comparison of early copies to determine wording that most closely represents the original writings. Many of the popular translations (e.g. King James Version, New American Standard Version, New International Version, English Standard Version, etc.) are translated from accurate Greek texts by groups of outstanding linguistic scholars. They have studied each word and verse in the languages of the originals in order to bring to us an English Bible that most closely represents the original wording and meaning of God's Word.

The "original" Scriptural writings are no longer available, but there are thousands of copies of the originals that give clear indications that the true text of Scripture we have today is indeed God's Word.

"There is in the National Archive Building in Washington, D.C. that contains the original document of the United States Constitution. It is a valuable national treasure and is carefully guarded in a fireproof vault. Thousands view it every year. Yet if the original should be stolen or destroyed, the government would not collapse, for there are sufficient copies in existence to demonstrate what the original document said. In the same way the thousands of biblical ancient manuscripts in existence have preserved the contents of the autographs beyond any reasonable doubt."[1]

---

[1] Dr. Homer Kent, Former President/Professor of Grace Theological Seminary

Session 1: *The Bible*

The Bible is unique among all other books. God used about forty men over a period of approximately 1,500 years to write His Word for mankind. Though the Scriptures are God's Word, the human authors did not write by dictation. God was at work in these men, using their own minds, languages, backgrounds and experiences to communicate the exact words God predetermined to use in writing His truths for mankind.

7.1 According to 2 Peter 1:20-21, where has the Scripture originated or come from?

7.2 According to 2 Peter 1:20-21, who was the driving force (i.e. "carried men along") as they wrote the Scripture?

8.1 According to Titus 1:2, Hebrews 6:18, and 1 John 2:21, does God lie?

8.2 According to John 17:17, what is Truth?

8.3 Since the Bible is God's Word, and God does not lie, can we have confidence in what the Bible says? Explain.

9.1 According to James 1:22-25, what should we do when we understand what God is saying through the Bible?

9.2 What happens if we do not obey?

9.3 What happens if we do obey?

Session 1: *The Bible*

notes

Session 2: *The One True God*

> **The One True God:** There is but one true God existing eternally as three persons: God the Father, God the Son, and God the Holy Spirit. All three Persons of the Godhead are co-equal and the same in essence but distinct in subsistence (Luke 3:22; Matthew 28:19; 2 Corinthians 13:14).

1.0 Look up and read the following verses: Deuteronomy 6:4; Isaiah 44:6; and James 2:19. According to these verses, how many true gods are there?

2.1 Read Exodus 20:1-6. What do you think God's attitude is toward idolatry?

2.2 Idolatry could be defined as "excessive attachment to some person or thing." According to Colossians 3:5, excessive attachment to what is a form of idolatry for the Christian? What are some "idols" that people often have in their lives?

Session 2: *The One True God*

3.0 Fill-in-the-blank: "In the beginning God created the heavens and the earth" (Genesis 1:1). Look up the following words in a Bible Dictionary (or Webster's Dictionary) and fill in the appropriate blanks with: *atheism, evolution, fatalism, materialism, pantheism,* **and** *polytheism.*

a. "In the beginning **God**..." – that denies _____, with its doctrine of no God.

b. "In the beginning **God**..." – that denies _____, with its doctrine of many gods.

c. "In the beginning God **created**..." – that denies _____, with its doctrine of chance to change from simple to complex.

d. "In the beginning **God created**..." – that denies _____, with its doctrine that all events are predetermined and unalterable.

e. "In the beginning **God created the heavens and the earth**." – that denies _____, with its doctrine that the universe is God.

f. "In the beginning God **created the heavens and the earth**." – that denies _____, with its doctrine that matter is eternal.

Session 2: *The One True God*

    The Bible has the presupposition that God exists. After all, since God is God, He doesn't need to "prove" Himself. He is eternal, without beginning or end. He has no origin! This is a strange concept to our finite minds where everything we encounter has both a beginning and end. Yet God has neither. He has always existed. He is eternal.
    Many skeptics may challenge believers by asking for proof of God's existence. This should not be intimidating. Though we can't see God, He has provided ample evidences of His existence. The question is not whether God exists; but rather, will we choose to believe the evidence God has provided.

4.0   According to Psalm 19:1, what do the heavens declare?

5.0   According to Romans 1:20, why don't men have any excuses for not believing in God?

6.0   In addition to creation, there are other avenues God has used to reveal Himself to man. Read the following verses and write down some of the ways that God reveals Himself.

    1 Corinthians 11:7 with Genesis 1:26-27; 9:6 –

    Exodus 7:3, 5; 13:1 with Acts 2:17–

    2 Peter 2:15-16 with Numbers 22:28 –

    John 8:27, 28, 38; 12:39 –

    John 20:30-31 –

    Acts 2:3, 4, 11 with 1 Corinthians 14 –

    Acts 9:4-7 –

    Hebrews 1:1-3 –

7.0   How do you think God has chosen to clearly reveal Himself today (i.e. what is God's Word in this day and age)?

Session 2: *The One True God*

Another strange and difficult concept for our finite mind is the biblical teaching of the tri-unity of God (commonly called the trinity). This teaching states that there is one true God existing as three separate persons for all eternity.

People can comprehend that there is only one true God. In fact, every Jewish boy used to learn and memorize the "Shema," the Jewish foundational statement of Deuteronomy 6:4: "Hear, O Israel: The LORD our God, the LORD is one. Beside Him, there is no other" (Deuteronomy 4:35, 39).

It becomes confusing then, in the New Testament, when we discover that the Bible teaches that there are three Persons in the Godhead. How can God be three and one? This proves to be a most difficult concept. The tri-unity of God is a biblical teaching that must and can only be accepted by faith – not human reasoning.

8.0 **How many persons does Matthew 3:16-17; Luke 3:21-22; and Matthew 28:19 demonstrate that exist within the Godhead?**

The greatest picture of the triunity of God (i.e. the Trinity) is found in the ordinance of water baptism. Though we will discuss this ordinance at length in a later session, it may prove helpful to briefly describe how this pictures the triunity of God.

When someone is biblically baptized, they are to be immersed or dipped into the water three times. The water symbolically represents the very essence of God. Each dip symbolically represents a different Person in the Godhead (i.e. God the Father, God the Son, and God the Holy Spirit). Three dips... three Persons. Each Person's essence is identical as represented by the exact same substance used for each dip... H_2O. But there is only one complete baptism just as there is only one true God. Three dips yet one baptism which represents the Three Persons yet one God.

Session 2: *The One True God*

The attributes or qualities of God are not characteristics that man has assigned to God, but rather revelation that God has given about Himself in the Bible. Since God has clearly revealed Himself, mankind can come to know Him.

9.0 Match the attributes of God with the appropriate Scriptures:

_____ **Omnipotent** (all powerful)   A. Job 42:2a and Mark 10:27

_____ **Omniscient** (all knowing)   B. Psalm 139:7-12

_____ **Omnipresent** (everywhere)   C. Isaiah 55:9 and 1 John 3:20

_____ **Sovereign** (in control)   D. Matthew 10:29 and Eph 1:11

10. List at least one of the above attributes of God that may answer one of the following skeptic's statements.

a. "God will never know I did this."

b. "Why do bad things to happen to good people?"

c. "I need to go to a church to pray because God is there."

d. "I don't believe God could create everything in just six literal days."

God has many other attributes or qualities that He has revealed to us about His essence or nature. Some of these attributes are: eternal, incomprehensible, infinite, unchangeable, righteous, holy, just, merciful, self-existent, truthful, faithful, good, gracious, love, etc. Each of the three Persons of the Godhead independently and completely possesses all the attributes of Deity. It would be beyond the scope of this study to try and understand or exhaust all of God's attributes!

Session 2: *The One True God*

notes

Session 3: *God the Father*

> **God the Father:** A Person known as God the Father in the Godhead. Draws people unto himself (John 6:44); the author of that day and hour of the coming of the Son of Man (Matthew 24:36); raised Jesus Christ from the dead (Romans 6:4; Galatians 1:1; 1 Thes 1:10); exalted Jesus' name above all names (Philippians 2:9-11); the other two Persons of the Godhead, not being inferior in any way, are voluntarily subordinate to God the Father's Sovereign Will and Plan (John 8:28-29 and 16:5-15; Luke 22:42; Galatians 1:3-4 with 4:6; Ephesians 1:11-14).

1.0 According to John 6:44, what is the only way in which someone can come to Jesus Christ?

2.0 According to Matthew 24:36, who is the only person who knows the day and hour when Jesus Christ will return?

3.1 According to Romans 6:4 and Galatians 1:1, who raised Jesus Christ from the dead?

3.2 According to Romans 4:25, why was Jesus raised from the dead?

Session 3: *God the Father*

The Particular Works of the Father

Almost everything God does in some way involve each Person of the Trinity. So when we speak of the particular works of the Father we are not excluding the other Persons, but simply delineating those things which seem to be the prerogative of the Father in a special way. Much like Jesus was the Person who died on the cross... not the Father or the Holy Spirit. But all three Persons of the Godhead were directly involved in the event.

1. *It is the Father who was the Author of the decree or plan of God (Psalms 2:7–9).*
2. *The Father was related to the act of election as its Author (Ephesians 1:3–6).*
3. *The Father raised Jesus from the dead (Romans 6:4; Galatians 1:1; 1 Thessalonians 1:10).*
4. *The Father sent the Son to this world (John 5:37).*
5. *The Father is the disciplinarian of His children (Hebrews 12:9).*[2]

4.1 **According to Philippians 2:9-11 (along with 1 Corinthians 15:27), who exalted Jesus Christ to the highest place?**

4.2 **What will every person who has ever existed do and to who's glory?**

5.0 **According to Luke 22:42 and John 8:28-29, how does Jesus decide what He does and says?**

---

[2]Ryrie, Charles Caldwell: *A Survey of Bible Doctrine*. Chicago : Moody Press, 1995

Session 3: *God the Father*

6.1 Who does the pronoun "him" and "his" refer to in Ephesians 1:11?

6.2 According to Ephesians 1:11-14, whose plan/will is being carried out?

7.0 TRUE or FALSE. If someone submits to someone else they are inferior; therefore, Jesus Christ is a little less than God the Father and the Holy Spirit is inferior to Jesus Christ. (hint: consider the God-ordained institution of marriage along with 1 Corinthians 14:33 to help answer this question)?

8.0 A person or personality is defined as having characteristics or personality traits such as: will, intellect, emotion, living, spirit, etc. Every Person in the Godhead possesses all of the attributes of Deity as well as Personality. Match the following Scriptures with the appropriate Personality traits attributed to God the Father.

____ John 6:57   A. will

____ Lk 22:42 and 2 Tim. 1:1   B. intellect/wisdom

____ Acts 1:7   C. emotion/love

____ John 4:21-24   D. living

____ 1 John 3:1 with Ps 79:5   E. spirit

____ 1 Corinthians 1:18-25   F. self-awareness

Session 3: *God the Father*

notes

Session 4: *God the Son*

> **God the Son:** A Person known as God the Son in the Godhead; that is, Jesus Christ. His preexistence and deity (John 1:1-3); incarnation by virgin birth (John 1:14; Matthew 1:18-23); sinless life (Hebrews 4:15); substitutionary death (2 Corinthians 5:21); bodily resurrection after being in the tomb three days and three nights (Luke 24:36-43 with Matthew 12:40); ascension into heaven and present ministry (Hebrews 4:14-16), and coming again (Acts 1:11).

1.1 Who does John 1:1-2 claim is God? According to John 1:1-18, to whom does this refer?

1.2 According to John 1:1-2, how long has Jesus existed?

2.0 What has the Son of God done according to John 1:3 and Colossians 1:16?

3.1 What did Jesus say in John 8:56-59?

3.2 What does this mean?

3.3 Why and how did the Jews respond to Jesus' claim?

4.0 How and why did the Jews respond to what Jesus said in John 10:30 (John 10:31 – 33)?

Session 4: *God the Son*

5.1 According to John 5:22-23, how much honor did Jesus say should be given to Him?

5.2 According to Philippians 2:10-11, what will every single human being do?

6.1 According to the 2 of the Ten Commandments in Exodus 20:4-6, and what Jesus said in Matthew 4:8-10, who alone should be worshipped?

6.2 Read Matthew 2:11, 14:33, 28:9; Luke 24:52; and John 9:38. Did these people break the 2 Commandment? Explain.

7.0 List the works that Jesus does that only God alone can do.

    a. Luke 5:20-24:

    b. John 1:3, 10; Colossians 1:16; Hebrews 1:10:

    c. John 5:21, 28, 29:

    d. John 5:22-27:

    e. Colossians 1:17; Hebrews 1:3:

8.0 According to Matthew 1:18-25, what was unusual about Jesus' mother and her conception?

Session 4: *God the Son*

9.1 How many times had Jesus sinned (Hebrews 4:15)?

9.2 According to Romans 3:23, how many other people have never sinned?

9.3 According to Romans 6:23, what is the just due penalty (i.e. wages) for sinning?

9.4 Did Jesus deserve this penalty?

9.5 Do you deserve this penalty?

10.0 According to Romans 5:7-8; 1 Peter 3:18a; 1 John 4:9-10; and 2 Corinthians 5:21, how has Jesus' death affected us?

11.0 TRUE or FALSE. According to Hebrews 4:14-16; 7:23-25; 1 John 2:1; and John 14:1-3; after Jesus ascended into heaven (Acts 1:9-11), He left the *sole* responsibility of ministering to believers to the Holy Spirit.

12.1 According to Matthew 12:40; 28:1-20; Luke 24:1-53; Acts 1:3; 1 Corinthians 15:5-8; and 1 Peter 3:18-19, what happened to Christ after he had died on the cross?

12.2 How long was Jesus Christ in the tomb (Matthew 12:40)?

12.3 What day was the tomb discovered empty (Matthew 28:1; Mark 16:1-2; Luke 24:1)?

Session 4: *God the Son*

13.0 *Jesus Christ is coming again! Christ's second coming is mentioned 318 times in the 210 chapters of the New Testament. It was, and is, the most looked for coming event in all of church history! The events surrounding His second coming will be dealt with in greater detail in Session 12, THE SECOND COMING.* **Match the following descriptions with the appropriate Scriptures that indicate that Christ will indeed return from heaven again (i.e. His imminent return):**

_____ Matthew 16:27   A. It will be unexpected

_____ Revelation 1:7   B. It will be sudden

_____ John 14:3-4   C. It will be with God's Glory

_____ Acts 1:11   D. It will be visible – every eye will see

_____ 1 Corinthians 15:51-52   E. It will be literal

_____ Luke 17:26-29 and   F. It will be personal – to
        1 Thessalonians 5:2-3   take us where He is

Session 5: *God the Holy Spirit*

> **God the Holy Spirit:** A Person known as God the Holy Spirit in the Godhead. His personality (John 16:7-15); and Deity (Acts 5:3-4); and His present work in each believer: baptism at the moment of regeneration (1 Corinthians 12:13), indwelling at the moment of regeneration (Romans 8:9), to teach and remind believers all that Christ has said (John 14:26).

It is not hard for most people to understand that God the Father is Deity (i.e. God). It is often more difficult for people to grasp that God the Father is a Person in the Godhead. And since the beginning of the church, believers have often struggled with the hypostatic union of Jesus Christ (i.e. Christ being 100% human and 100% God). And with the Holy Spirit, many believers struggle with His personhood. He is not an "it." He is a Person in the Godhead. He is Deity. There is only one true living God eternally existing as three Persons – God the Father, God the Son, and God the Holy Spirit!

1.0 **Match the following Scriptures with the appropriate Personality traits of God the Holy Spirit:**

____ Ephesians 4:30 and Romans 15:30   A. He has a will

____ Romans 8:11 and Hebrews 9:14   B. We can have fellowship with Him

____ 2 Corinthians 13:14 Philippians 2:1-2   C. He has emotion

____ John 3:6 and 1 Corinthians 2:10-14   D. He is living

____ Acts 16:6-7 and 1 Corinthians 12:11   E. He is spirit

____ Acts 15:8 1 Corinthians 2:10-11   F. He has intellect (i.e. He knows the thoughts of man and God)

Session 5: *God the Holy Spirit*

Upon regeneration (i.e. receiving Christ, being born again, becoming a Christian, etc.), the Holy Spirit ministers in several ways to people. Both Jesus and the Holy Spirit baptizes believers. The word baptize means to completely saturate or immerse as to identify. For example, someone could be baptized, or immersed, in fear; therefore, the person is completely consumed of fear (the word baptize will be discussed in greater detail in Session 11). He also indwells every believer. The word "indwell" means to live with or take residence. At the point of regeneration, the Holy Spirit takes permanent residence or lives in the believer. And finally, the Holy Spirit is deposited within the believer. The Holy Spirit is a deposit guaranteeing what God has promised and assures that the believer can never be cut off from God.

2.0 **Write the appropriate letter next to the following verses:**

    B = baptism   I = indwell   R = rebirth   S = seal

_____ John 3:3-5

_____ Romans 8:9

_____ 1 Corinthians 3:16 and 6:19

_____ 1 Corinthians 12:13

_____ 2 Corinthians 1:21-22

_____ Ephesians 1:13-14

_____ Ephesians 4:4-5

_____ Titus 3:5

Session 5: *God the Holy Spirit*

In John 14:26 Christ states: "But the Helper, the Holy Spirit, whom the Father will send in my name, he will **teach** you and **remind** you all that I have said to you." *(emphasis mine)*

3.0 According to the above verse, what will the Holy Spirit teach?

4.0 According to the above verse, what will the Holy Spirit remind believers?

5.0 Read 1 Corinthians 2:9-16.

    verse 10a. What has God revealed to us by the Holy Spirit?

    verse 10b. What does the Holy Spirit search?

    verse 11. Who knows the thoughts of God?

    verse 12a. What Spirit have believers received?

    verse 12b. What does that allow believers to understand?

    verse 13. What does the Holy Spirit interpret to whom?

    verse 14. Can someone who has not been baptized or indwelt by the Holy Spirit understand God's Word? Why or Why not?

    verse 15 and 16. What kind of mind does a believer have?

Session 5: *God the Holy Spirit*

notes

Session 6: *Satan*

> **Satan:** his existence and personality as the great adversary of God and His people (Revelation 12:1-10); his judgment (John 12:31); and final doom (Revelation 20:10).

1.1 **What were the first four words (according to the ESV translation) Satan said to mankind (Genesis 3:1)?**

1.2 **How long after creation, do you think it was before Satan fell and deceived Eve?**

God's Word is truth (John 17:17). It is the Truth of God (i.e. God's Word) that sets one free (John 8:32); renews one's mind and transforms the believer into the image of Christ (Romans 12:1-4). God's word is the life changing power for every believer.

2.0 **According to the following verses, what are some ways that Satan tries to diminish the power of God's Word in a believer's life?**

Genesis 3:1b

Luke 4:10-11

John 8:44

Revelation 20:7-10

Session 6: *Satan*

3.0 Often the names of individuals in the Bible describe something about their character, personality, or works. Match the following Bible references to the titles or names for Satan (e.g. Satan means adversary):

_____ Gen. 3:1-4, 13-14; Revelation 12:9   A. Father of lies (perverts truth)

_____ Matthew 4:3   B. Accuser (accuses believers)

_____ John 8:44b   C. Tempter (solicits people to sin)

_____ John 12:31   D. Serpent (deceiver)

_____ John 17:15; 1 John 2:14   E. The god of this world

_____ 2 Corinthians 4:4   F. Ruler of this world

_____ Hebrew 2:14   G. The evil one (intrinsically evil)

_____ 1 Peter 5:8   H. Devil (means slanderer)

_____ Revelation 12:10   I. Like a roaring lion (i.e. murderer… leads people to eternal death)

Session 6: *Satan*

Satan is the enemy of God. He is a created being who once had a place of great honor in God's heavenly courts. He was a beautiful, powerful, guardian angel. His name was Lucifer (now called Satan, which means "enemy of God"). However, his great wisdom and beauty made him proud. He desired to be like God and be worshipped by man (Isaiah 14:13-14). One third of all the angels followed Lucifer. The fallen angels are known as demons. Lucifer and his angels were cast down out of heaven and defeated. Even though Satan failed in his revolt, he is consistent in his character of opposing God and trying to thwart His plan.

4.0 **Since God is Omniscient (i.e. all knowing; therefore, He knew that Lucifer would rebel), why do you think He even created Satan in the first place** (note: you may want to consider Romans 9:21-23 and Ephesians 1:11-12)**?**

5.1 **How do most people picture the Devil?**

5.2 **How is Satan described in 2 Corinthians 11:13-15?**

Session 6: *Satan*

6.0 Studying the temptation of Jesus Christ by Satan can give us insight into Satan's strategies and schemes. Read Matthew 4:1-11 and then answer the following questions.

    a. What places did Satan tempt Jesus Christ?

    b. What were the circumstances when Satan tempted Jesus Christ?

    c. With what things did he try to tempt Jesus Christ?

    d. What did Satan quote to try and convince Jesus to sin?

    e. How did Jesus defend Himself against Satan's temptations?

Satan is a created angelic being in the order of angels called cherubim (Ezekiel 28:11-19). That means he does not possess attributes which belong to God alone, like omnipresence, omniscience, or omnipotence. Though a mighty being, he has creaturely limitations. And as a creature he must be accountable to his Creator.[3]

7.0 **TRUE or FALSE.** Satan is omnipresent... meaning he can be influencing you while he is influencing someone else half way around the world at the same time?

---

[3] Charles Ryrie, *Basic Theology*, page 138

Session 6: *Satan*

8.0 **TRUE or FALSE. Satan is omniscient... meaning he can read your mind and knows your every thought?**

9.0 **TRUE or FALSE. Satan is omnipotent... meaning his power has no limits except when God contains it.**

10.0 **When do you think Lucifer and all the angles were created** (hint: Exodus 20:11 with Job 38:4-7)**?**

11.0 **List all the "I will..." statements in Isaiah 14:13-14. Assuming this passage is a reference to Satan, why do you think Lucifer and a third of the angles were cast out of heaven?**

12.0 **According to Revelation 20:10, what is Satan's final doom?**

Session 6: *Satan*

notes

Session 7: *Humanity*

> **Humanity:** humanity's direct creation in the image of God (Genesis 1:26-28); humanity's subsequent fall into sin resulting in spiritual death (Genesis 3:1-24; Romans 5:12); humanity's every inclination of the thoughts of their heart is only evil all the time from conception until rebirth (Jeremiah 17:9; Romans 8:1-17; Galatians 5:16-26); the necessity of the new birth for their salvation (John 3:3-5); and the believer possessing two opposing natures while in this world (Romans 7:14-25; 8:1-18).

1.0 According to Genesis 1:24-31 and 2:7, answer the following:

    a. What day of creation did God create man?

    b. On what day and how did God create animals?

    c. How did God create Adam's body?

    d. When did Adam become a living being?

    e. In what likeness or image did God create man?

2.1 Who were the first, second, and third created beings to sin?

2.2 According to Genesis 3:1-24 and Romans 5:12, whose sin resulted in sin entering and affecting God's entire creation?

2.3 Why do you think this particular sin allowed sin to enter the world?

Session 7: *Humanity*

3.0   Read the following passages and write a definition of sin: Romans 3:23, 14:23; James 4:17; and 1 John 3:4, 5:17.

4.0   Why do humans sin (Jeremiah 17:9; James 1:14-15)?

5.0   According to Romans 5:12 with Psalm 51:5, where does this propensity, desire, or nature to sin come from?

6.0   According to Romans 3:23, how many people have sinned?

7.0   According to Romans 6:23, what does one deserve (i.e. earnings or wages) due to their sin?

The Bible teaches that every person is a sinner, and as a result, are on their way to judgment, punishment, and everlasting separation from God. God will judge sin because He is a holy and just God. He cannot just turn His back on sin and say, "I'll just forgive your sins if you do more good works than bad," or "Don't sin anymore and we'll call it even." Because of God's holiness a price for sin must be paid.

Because of God's great love, He chose to pay the price for the due penalty man deserves. Jesus Christ is the perfect payment for the forgiveness of man's sin. Even though Christ's payment was more than sufficient for the price of sin, each individual must personally apply this payment to his own debt owed to God (Romans 10:9-10).

Every human being has been conceived in sin and has inherited a sin nature. Every child of God has been born from above and inherited God's nature. Flesh gives birth to flesh, but Spirit gives birth to spirit. Every person must be spiritually born again, or born from above by God, in order to become a child of God.

Session 7: *Humanity*

8.0 According to John 3:3, what must happen in order for someone to enter the Kingdom of God?

9.1 According to John 1:12-13, how does someone become a child of God?

9.2 What do you think this means and how do you think this happens?

10.0 Carefully read Romans 7:14-25. The Apostle Paul refers to himself as possessing two natures: the spiritual nature (being born of God) and the natural or carnal nature (being born from Adam's race). Carefully read and then answer the following questions from Romans 7:14-25:

v. 15. Does the spiritual man do what he truly wants to do?

v. 15. What does the spiritual man end up doing?

v. 16. By the carnal nature doing what the spiritual nature does not want to do, what does this prove about the law (i.e. God's Word or God's Standard)?

v. 17. Does the spiritual nature of man cause one to sin?

Session 7: *Humanity*

10.0 **Carefully read Romans 7:14-25** (continued).

  v. 18. Is there anything good that lives in the carnal nature?

  v. 19. What does the Christian keep on doing?

  v. 20. Which nature does the pronoun "I" refer to in "…it is no longer I who do it…" (i.e. the carnal or spiritual nature)?

  v. 21. What is close at hand with the spiritual nature?

  v. 22. What does the spiritual nature delight in?

  v. 23. What is the carnal nature a prisoner to?

  v. 24, 25. Who can rescue the spiritual nature from this condition?

  v. 25. Which nature is a slave to sin and which is a slave to God?

Session 8: *Salvation*

> **Salvation:** a complete and eternal salvation by God's grace alone; received as the gift of God through faith according to His predetermined plan and purpose; one is completely justified by faith in God's Word alone (Ephesians 2:8-9; Titus 3:3-7; Genesis 15:6 with Romans 4:1-25; Romans 10:17 with Romans 1:16).

1.0 According to Romans 5:9, what have believers been saved from?

2.0 TRUE or FALSE (if the statement is false, rewrite the statement to make it true). Read Ephesians 2:8-9 to answer the following questions:

    _____ It is by grace *alone* that someone is saved.

    _____ God gives grace if one does good things.

    _____ Salvation is completely and solely a gift of God.

    _____ Salvation is based upon what individuals do.

    _____ Christians who have faith in the truth of the Bible, will be the only people (in our current time) that go to heaven.

3.0 If salvation required works on our part, what would that say about Christ's death, burial, and resurrection?

Session 8: *Salvation*

4.0 **MATCHING:** Match the scriptures with the appropriate statements:

_____ John 6:37   A. Absolutely nothing will be able to separate a Christian from God's love.

_____ John 10:27-29   B. Christ will never cast out or drive you away.

_____ Romans 8:38-39   C. A believer's hope of salvation can never perish and is guarded by God's power.

_____ 1 Peter 1:3-5   D. No one can snatch a believer out of God's hand.

5.0 Reread the preface of this study (pages iv – xxi). When, if ever, would you say you have crossed over the bridge, Jesus Christ, from death to life? Write down some details of this experience and be prepared to share your personal testimony.

Session 8: *Salvation*

> *"Everyone who believes in Jesus Christ with a true biblical faith immediately enters into all that divine love provides [i.e. eternal life]. These positions and possessions [Chafer names thirty-three] are not bestowed in succession, but simultaneously."*[4]

6.0 **From the following passages, list some of the many blessings that belong to believers upon regeneration (i.e. being born again, becoming a Christian, becoming a child of God, being saved, etc.).**

John 1:12 with Galatians 3:26:

Romans 5:1:

Romans 8:17:

Ephesians 1:7:

Philippians 3:20:

1 Peter 2:10:

---

[4] Lewis Sperry Chafer

Session 8: *Salvation*

7.0 **Matching:** Put the correct letter of the scripture reference that corresponds to the correct Soteriological doctrine (i.e. Soteriology means, "the study of salvation"). (Optional: For additional study, read the following theological definitions and articles and put the number of theological definition that corresponds to the correct Soteriological doctrine.)

Doctrine	Scripture Reference	Theological Definition
Conviction	_____	_____
Faith	_____	_____
Forgiveness	_____	_____
Glorification	_____	_____
Justification	_____	_____
Preservation	_____	_____
Propitiation	_____	_____
Reconciliation	_____	_____
Redemption	_____	_____
Regeneration	_____	_____
Repentance	_____	_____
Sanctification	_____	_____

Session 8: *Salvation*

Scripture References

A. Hebrews 11:1, 6; Ephesians 2:8-9; Romans 3:21-26; 10:17b

B. Romans 3:25; 1 John 4:10

C. John 10:27-30; Rom. 11:25-31; Philippians 1:3-6; 2 Tim. 1:8, 12

D. Romans 3:21-26; Galatians 2:15-21

E. Romans 8:17-18, 28-30; 1 Corinthians 15:42-44; Colossians 3:1-4

F. Ephesians 1:7; Galatians 3:13; 1 Peter 1:18-19

G. Romans 5:10-11; 2 Corinthians 5:16-21

H. John 16:7-11; 1 Thessalonians 1:4-5

I. 2 Peter 3:9; 2 Timothy 2:22-26; Romans 2:1-4; 2 Cor. 7:8-10

J. Titus 3:4-7; 1 Peter 1:23; John 3:3 with 1:12

K. Romans 4:4-8; 1 John 2:12

L. 1 Corinthians 1:2, 6:11; John 17:1-3, 16-19

Session 8: *Salvation*

Theological Definitions

1. The ransom or price fully paid, which is the death of Christ through the shedding of His blood, necessary to purchase the individual by paying the debt owed to God by sinful man in order to free sinners from the bondage of sin and the resulting curse imposed by the law.

2. The believer used to be an enemy of God, but because of the death of Jesus, the Christian's relationship with God is changed for the better. This changed relationship is not the result of our own efforts or performance; it is exclusively the result of God's work in Christ.

3. The forgiving mercy and turning away of the deserved wrath of a just and Holy God due to the sacrifice and/or offering of Jesus Christ.

4. A ministry of the Holy Spirit which gives convincing illuminating proof of the truth of the Christian message.

5. A genuine, not superficial, change of mind, to have another mind, about face, or turning from belief in other things and turning to God. Having a changed mind toward God that is followed by some kind of change in action.

6. A certain conviction, wrought in the heart by the Holy Spirit, as to the truth of the gospel, and a hearty reliance (trust) on the promises of God in Christ as proclaimed in His Word.

7. An inner re-creating, or new birth, of fallen human nature by the gracious sovereign action of the Holy Spirit, which the new creation receives a new nature, no longer conformed to this world, but in knowledge and holiness of the truth is reflected and created after the image of God.

Session 8: *Salvation*

Theological Definitions (continued)

8. To pardon as to cancel or remit a debt by relinquishing all rights and desire to justly punish or exact penalty for an offense. This doctrine is one of the constituent parts of justification. In pardoning sin, God absolves the sinner from the condemnation of the law, and that on account of the work of Christ, he removes the guilt of sin, or the sinner's actual liability to eternal wrath on account of it.

9. A direct action initiated by God on the individual which grants the forgiveness and total elimination of a believer's sin declaring or making a sinner righteous before God on the grounds of Jesus' imputed righteousness and shed blood at his crucifixion. God's act of making a sinner righteous before Him by His grace, received through the faith given to the person by God, for Christ's sake, because of his life, death, and resurrection.

10. God will continue the work He has begun in the believer until He brings it to completion.

11. That continuous operation of the Holy Spirit in the believer, by which the work of divine grace that is begun in the heart, is continued and brought to completion. The believer is set apart by God to do a holy work for His glory.

12. The receiving of perfection by the elect before entering into the kingdom of heaven, and the receiving of the resurrection bodies by the elect.

Session 8: *Salvation*

notes

Session 8: *Salvation*

Table of Contents of Theological Terms

Conviction .... page 85

Forgiveness .... page 85

Faith .... page 86

Glorification .... page 93

Justification .... page 97

Preservation .... page 100

Propitiation .... page 109

Reconciliation .... page 112

Redemption .... page 113

Regeneration .... page 113

Repentance .... page 117

Sanctification .... page 119

Conviction

Conviction is the work of the Holy Spirit within an individual (John 16:8). A conviction is often defined as a strongly held belief; however, in the theological sense, the word conviction embraces a number of biblical expressions in its meaning. Originally it derived from two Latin terms meaning "cause to see." The New Testament uses the terms reproof, conviction, and illumination to communicate the ministry of the Holy Spirit whereby He causes the individual to "see" (understand) truth. The illumination of the Holy Spirit is the process by which God's Holy Spirit enables us to understand His word and apply it to our lives (1 Corinthians 2:12-14; 1 John 2:20, 27). (It should be noted that the dependency every believer has upon the Holy Spirit to illuminate the truth of the Scriptures does in no way diminish the perspicuity or clarity of the Scriptures.) But once the truth is illuminated to the believer via the Holy Spirit, this truth becomes an inseparable part of the inner spirit of the individual that it becomes a definitive part of their being. This is where the conviction of the believer is birthed. The truth is so vividly realized that the Christian's way of life is submissively obliged to follow their conviction.

Forgiveness

One of the constituent parts of justification. In pardoning sin, God absolves the sinner from the condemnation of the law, and that on account of the work of Christ; he removes the guilt of sin, or the sinner's actual liability to eternal wrath on account of it. All sins are forgiven freely (Acts 5:31; 13:38; 1 John 1:6-9). The sinner is by this act of grace for ever freed from the guilt and penalty of his sins. This is the peculiar prerogative of God (Ps. 130:4; Mark 2:5). It is offered to all in the gospel.

Session 8: *Salvation*

Faith

Faith is in general the persuasion of the mind that a certain statement is true (Philippians 1:27; 2 Thessalonians 2:13). Its primary idea is trust. A thing is true, and therefore worthy of trust. It admits of many degrees up to full assurance of faith, in accordance with the evidence on which it rests.

Faith is the result of hearing God's word (Romans 10:14-17). Knowledge is an essential element in all faith, and is sometimes spoken of as an equivalent to faith (John 10:38; 1 John 2:3). Yet the two are distinguished in this respect, that faith includes in it assent, which is an act of the will in addition to the act of the understanding. Assent to the truth is of the essence of faith, and the ultimate ground on which our assent to any revealed truth rests is the veracity (truthfulness or accuracy) of God.

Viewed more particularly with reference to its intellectual aspect, faith is properly defined as the conviction of the reality of the truths and facts which God has revealed, such conviction resting solely upon the testimony of God.

There is an element that is intellectual; also an element, of even deeper importance, that is moral. Faith is not simply the assent of the intellect to revealed truth; it is the practical submission of the entire man to the guidance and control of such truth, "The devils believe and tremble". Thus in its beginning and completion faith is one of the fruits of the Spirit (Galatians 5:22).

Romans 4:13-22 (Abraham received the promise through the righteousness of faith). The promise was made to Abraham long before the law. It points at Christ, and it refers to the promise, Genesis 12:3. In Thee shall all families of the earth be blessed. The law worketh wrath, by showing that every transgressor is exposed to the Divine displeasure. As God intended to give men a title to the promised blessings, so he appointed it to be by faith, that it might be wholly of grace, to make it sure to all who were of the like precious faith with Abraham, whether Jews or Gentiles, in all ages. The justification and salvation of sinners, the taking to himself the Gentiles

Session 8: *Salvation*

who had not been a people, were a gracious calling of things which are not, as though they were; and this giving a being to things that were not, proves the almighty power of God.   The nature and power of Abraham's faith are shown. He believed God's testimony, and looked for the performance of his promise, firmly hoping when the case seemed hopeless. It is weakness of faith, that makes a man lie poring on the difficulties in the way of a promise. Abraham took it not for a point that would admit of argument or debate. Unbelief is at the bottom of all our staggerings at God's promises. The strength of faith appeared in its victory over fears.   God honours faith; and great faith honours God. It was imputed to him for righteousness. Faith is a grace that of all others gives glory to God.   Faith clearly is the instrument by which we receive the righteousness of God, the redemption which is by Christ; and that which is the instrument whereby we take or receive it, cannot be the thing itself, nor can it be the gift thereby taken and received.   Abraham's faith did not justify him by its own merit or value, but as giving him a part in Christ. (Matthew Henry's commentary).

Faith…
1. Is the substance of things hoped for. Hebrews 11:1
2. Is the evidence of things not seen. Hebrews 11:1
3. Commanded. Matthew 11:22; 1 John 3:23

In Christ Faith Is…
1. The gift of God. Romans 12:3; Eph. 2:8; Eph. 6:23; Phil. 1:29
2. The work of God. Acts 11:21; 1 Cor. 2:5
3. Precious. 2 Peter 1:1
4. Most holy. Jude 1:20
5. Fruitful. 1 Thes. 1:3
6. Accompanied by repentance. Mark 1:15; Luke 24:47
7. Followed by conversion. Acts 11:21

Session 8: *Salvation*

Obtained Through Faith…

1. Salvation. (Mark 16:16; Acts 16:31; Ephesians 2:8)
2. Remission of sins. (Acts 10:43; Romans 3:25)
3. Justification. (Acts 13:39; Rom 3:21-22, 28, 30; 5:1; Gal 2:16)
4. Sanctification. (Acts 15:9; Acts 26:18)
5. Spiritual light. (John 12:36, 46)
6. Spiritual life. (John 20:31; Galatians 2:20)
7. Eternal life. (John 3:15-16; John 6:40, 47)
8. Rest in heaven.(Hebrews 4:3)
9. Edification. (1 Timothy 1:4; Jude 1:20)
10. Preservation. (1 Peter 1:5)
11. Adoption. (John 1:12; Galatians 3:26)
12. Access to God. (Romans 5:2; Ephesians 3:12)
13. Inheritance of the promises. (Galatians 3:22; Hebrews 6:12)
14. The gift of the Holy Spirit. (Acts 11:15-17; Galatians 3:14; Ephesians 1:13)
15. Hope. (Romans 5:2)
16. Joy. (Acts 16:34; 1 Peter 1:8)
17. Peace. (Romans 15:13)
18. Confidence. (Isaiah 28:16; 1 Peter 2:6)
19. Boldness in preaching. (Psalm 116:10; 2 Corinthians 4:13)

Session 8: *Salvation*

By Faith Saints…

1. Live. (Galatians 2:20)
2. Stand. (Romans 11:20; 2 Corinthians 1:24)
3. Walk. (Romans 4:12; 2 Corinthians 5:7)
4. Obtain a good report. (Hebrews 11:2)
5. Overcome the world. (1 John 5:4-5)
6. Resist the devil. (1 Peter 5:9)
7. Overcome the devil. (Ephesians 6:16)
8. Are supported. (Psalm 27:13; 1 Timothy 4:10)

Saints Should…

1. Be sincere in faith. (1 Timothy 1:5; 2 Timothy 1:5)
2. Abound in faith. 2 Corinthians 8:7)
3. Continue in faith. (Acts 14:22; Colossians 1:23)
4. Be strong in faith. (Romans 4:20-24)
5. Stand fast in faith. (1 Corinthians 16:13)
6. Be grounded and settled in faith. (Colossians 1:23)
7. Hold, with a good conscience faith. (1 Timothy 1:19)
8. Pray for the increase of faith. (Luke 17:5)
9. Have full assurance of faith. (Hebrews 10:22; 2 Timothy 1:12)

Session 8: *Salvation*

Implications of Faith...

1. Impossible to please God without. (Hebrews 11:6)
2. Christ dwells in the heart by. (Ephesians 3:17)
3. Essential to the profitable reception of the gospel. Hebrews 4:2
4. Christ is the Author and Finisher of. (Hebrews 12:2)
5. Is a gift of the Holy Spirit. (1 Corinthians 12:9)
6. The Scriptures designed to produce. (John 20:31; 2 Timothy 3:15)
7. Preaching designed to produce. (John 17:20; Acts 8:12; Romans 10:14-15; Romans 10:17)
8. Necessary in prayer. (Matthew 21:22; James 1:6)
9. Necessary in the Christian warfare. (1 Timothy 1:18-19; 1 Timothy 6:12)
10. Excludes self-justification. (Romans 10:3-4)
11. Excludes boasting. (Romans 3:27)
12. Works by love. (Galatians 5:6; 1 Timothy 1:5; Philemon 1:5)
13. Christ is precious to those having. (1 Peter 2:7)
14. The gospel effectual in those who have. (1 Thessalonians 2:13)
15. An evidence of the new birth. (1 John 5:1)
16. Saints die in. (Hebrews 11:13)
17. True, evidenced by its fruits. (James 2:21-25)
18. Without fruits, is dead. (James 2:17, 20, 26)
19. Examine whether you be in. (2 Corinthians 13:5)
20. All difficulties overcome by. (Matthew 17:20; Matthew 21:21; Mark 9:23)

Session 8: *Salvation*

21. All things should be done in. (Romans 14:22)

22. Whatever is not of, is sin. (Romans 14:23)

23. Often tried by affliction. (1 Peter 1:6-7)

24. Trial of, works patience. (James 1:3)

25. The wicked often profess. (Acts 8:13-21)

26. The wicked destitute of. (John 10:25; John 12:37; Acts 19:9; 2 Thessalonians 3:2)

27. Protection of, illustrated; A shield. (Ephesians 6:16; A breastplate. 1 Thessalonians 5:8)

Faith Exemplified...

1. Caleb. (Numbers 13:30)

2. Job. (Job 19:25)

3. Shadrach. (Daniel 3:17)

4. Daniel. (Daniel 6:10, 23)

5. Peter. (Matthew 16:16)

6. Woman who was a sinner. (Luke 7:50)

7. Nathanael. (John 1:49)

8. Samaritans. (John 4:39)

9. Martha. (John 11:27)

10. The Disciples. (John 16:30)

11. Thomas. (John 20:28)

12. Stephen. (Acts 6:5)

Session 8: *Salvation*

13. Priests. (Acts 6:7)

14. Ethiopian. (Acts 8:37)

15. Barnabas. (Acts 11:24)

16. Sergius Paulus. (Acts 13:12)

17. Philippian jailor. (Acts 16:31, 34)

18. Romans. (Romans 1:8)

19. Colossians. (Colossians 1:4)

20. Thessalonians. (1 Thessalonians 1:3)

21. Lois. (2 Timothy 1:5)

22. Paul. (2 Timothy 4:7)

23. Abel. (Hebrews 11:4)

24. Enoch. (Hebrews 11:5)

25. Noah. (Hebrews 11:7)

26. Abraham. (Hebrews 11:8, 17)

27. Isaac. (Hebrews 11:20)

28. Jacob. (Hebrews 11:21)

29. Joseph. (Hebrews 11:22)

30. Moses. (Hebrews 11:24, 27)

31. Rahab. (Hebrews 11:31)

32. Gideon. (Hebrews 11:32-33, 39)

Session 8: *Salvation*

Glorification

There are two events that occur during glorification, these are "the receiving of perfection by the elect before entering into the kingdom of heaven," and "the receiving of the resurrection bodies by the elect"

Glorification is the future and final work of God upon Christians, where he transforms our mortal physical bodies to the eternal physical bodies in which we will dwell forever.

1 Corinthians 15:42-44, "So also is the resurrection of the dead. It is sown a perishable body, it is raised an imperishable body; it is sown in dishonor, it is raised in glory; it is sown in weakness, it is raised in power; it is sown a natural body, it is raised a spiritual body. If there is a natural body, there is also a spiritual body."

Jesus is the first resurrected from the dead in a glorified body. He is called the first fruits of creation. 1 Corinthians 15:20 says, "But now Christ has been raised from the dead, the first fruits of those who are asleep." Since he is the first fruits, we will follow. His resurrection is the promise and guarantee of our future resurrection.

In describing the attributes of resurrected bodies, we can derive certain qualities from the appearances of Christ after his resurrection. He retained the open wounds of his crucifixion (John 20:27-28), and therefore probably had no functioning circulatory system and would not need to eat - though he was able to eat. Since the wounds were still open, if blood circulation were still occurring it would have been expelled from the body through the wounds. So, apparently there is no need for functioning blood in the resurrected bodies.

Also, Jesus had the ability to simply appear and disappear at will. Mark 16:14 says, "And afterward He appeared to the eleven themselves as they were reclining at the table..." In John 20:27 we find, "And after eight days again His disciples were inside, and Thomas with them. Jesus came, the doors having been shut, and stood in their midst, and said, "Peace be with you." Therefore, we can

Session 8: *Salvation*

conclude that we will be able to do the same. Finally, death has no power over Jesus, so it will have no power over us in our new bodies and we will live forever, healthy, without being subject to death again.

1 Corinthians 15:51-53, "Behold, I tell you a mystery; we shall not all sleep, but we shall all be changed, in a moment, in the twinkling of an eye, at the last trumpet; for the trumpet will sound, and the dead will be raised imperishable, and we shall be changed. For this perishable must put on the imperishable, and this mortal must put on immortality."

The short answer is that "glorification" is God's final removal of sin from the life of the saints (i.e., everyone who is saved) in the eternal state (Romans 8:18; 2 Corinthians 4:17). At Christ's coming, the glory of God (Romans 5:2) – His honor, praise, majesty, and holiness-- will be realized in us; instead of being mortals burdened with sin nature, we will be changed into holy immortals with direct and unhindered access to God's presence, and we will enjoy holy commune with Him throughout eternity. In considering glorification, we should focus on Christ, for He is every Christian's "blessed hope"; also, we may consider final glorification as the culmination of sanctification.

Final glorification must await the manifestation of the glory of our great God and Savior Jesus Christ (Titus 2:13; 1 Timothy 6:14). Until He returns, we are burdened with sin, and our spiritual vision is distorted because of the curse. "For now we see in a mirror dimly, but then face to face. Now I know in part; then I shall know fully, even as I have been fully known" (1 Corinthians 13:12). Every day, we should be diligent by the Spirit to put to death what is earthly in us (Romans 8:13).

How and when will we be finally glorified? At the last trumpet, when Jesus comes, the saints will undergo a fundamental, instant transformation ("we shall all be changed, in a moment, in the twinkling of an eye" – 1 Corinthians 15:51); then our perishable bodies will put on imperishable immortality (1 Corinthians 15:53). Yet 2 Corinthians 3:18 clearly indicates that, in a mysterious sense, "we

Session 8: *Salvation*

all," in the present, "with unveiled face" are "beholding the glory of the Lord" and are being transformed into His image "from one degree of glory to another" (2 Corinthians 3:18). Lest anyone imagine that this beholding and transformation (as part of sanctification) is the work of especially saintly people, the Scripture adds the following caveat: "For this comes from the Lord who is the Spirit." In other words, it is a blessing bestowed on every believer. This does not refer to our final glorification, but to an aspect of sanctification by which the Spirit is transfiguring us right now. To Him be the praise for His work in sanctifying us in the Spirit and in truth (Jude 24-25; John 17:17; 4:23).

We should understand what Scripture teaches about the nature of glory – both God's unsurpassed glory and our share in it at His coming. God's glory refers not merely to the unapproachable light that the Lord inhabits (1 Timothy 6:15-16), but also to His honor (Luke 2:13) and holiness. The "You" referred to in Psalm 104:2 is the same God referenced in 1 Timothy 6:15-16; He is "clothed with splendor and majesty," covering Himself "with light as with a garment" (Psalm 104:2; cf. 93:1; Job 37:22; 40:10). When the Lord Jesus returns in His great glory to execute judgment (Matthew 24:29-31; 25:31-35), He will do so as the only Sovereign, who alone has eternal dominion (1 Timothy 6:14-16).

Created beings dare not gaze upon God's awesome glory; like Ezekiel (1:4-29) and Simon Peter (Luke 5:8), Isaiah was undone, devastated by self-loathing in the presence of the all-holy God. After the seraphim proclaimed, "Holy, holy, holy is the Lord of hosts; the whole earth is full of his glory!" Isaiah said, "Woe is me! For I am lost; for I am a man of unclean lips, and I dwell in the midst of a people of unclean lips; for my eyes have seen the King, the Lord of hosts!" (Isaiah 6:4). Even the seraphim showed that they were unworthy to gaze upon the divine glory, covering their faces with their wings.

God's glory may be said to be "heavy" or "weighty"; the Hebrew word *kabod* literally means "heavy or burdensome"; Most often, the Scriptural usage of *kabod* is figurative (e.g., "heavy with sin"), from

Session 8: *Salvation*

which we get the idea of the "weightiness" of a person who is honorable, impressive, or worthy of respect.

When the Lord Jesus became incarnate, He revealed both the "weighty" holiness of God and the fullness of His grace and truth ("and the Word became flesh and dwelt among us, and we have seen his glory, glory as of the only Son from the Father, full of grace and truth" John 1:14; cf. 17:1–5). The glory revealed by the incarnate Christ accompanies the ministry of the Spirit (2 Corinthians 3:7); it is unchanging and permanent (Isaiah 4:6-7; cf. Job 14:2; Psalm 102:11; 103:15; James 1:10). The previous manifestations of God's glory were temporary, like the fading effluence of God's glory from Moses' face. Moses veiled his face so that the hard-hearted Israelites might not see that the glory was fading (1 Corinthians 3:12), but in our case, the veil has been removed through Christ, and we reflect the glory of the Lord and seek by the Spirit to be like Him.

In His high priestly prayer, the Lord Jesus requested that God would sanctify us in His truth (i.e., make us holy; John 17:17); sanctification is necessary if we are to see Jesus' glory and be with Him in eternal fellowship (John 17:21-24). "Father, I desire that they also, whom you have given me, may be with me where I am, to see my glory that you have given me because you loved me before the foundation of the world (John 17:24). If the glorification of the saints follows the pattern revealed in Scripture, it must entail our sharing in the glory (i.e., the holiness) of God.

According to Philippians 3:20–21, our citizenship is in heaven, and when our Savior returns He will transform our lowly bodies "to be like His glorious body." Although it has not yet been revealed what we shall be, we know that, when He returns in great glory, we shall be like Him, for we shall see Him as He is (1 John 3:2). We will be perfectly conformed to the image of our Lord Jesus and be like Him in that our humanity will be free from sin and its consequences. Our blessed hope should spur us on to holiness, the Spirit enabling us. "Everyone who thus hopes in Him purifies himself as He is pure" (1 John 3:3).

Session 8: *Salvation*

Justification

A forensic term, opposed to condemnation. As regards its nature, it is the judicial act of God, by which he pardons all the sins of those who believe in Christ, and accounts, accepts, and treats them as righteous in the eye of the law, i.e., as conformed to all its demands. In addition to the pardon of sin, justification declares that all the claims of the law are satisfied in respect of the justified. It is the act of a judge and not of a sovereign. The law is not relaxed or set aside, but is declared to be fulfilled in the strictest sense; and so the person justified is declared to be entitled to all the advantages and rewards arising from perfect obedience to the law (Romans 5:1-10).

It proceeds on the imputing or crediting to the believer by God himself of the perfect righteousness, active and passive, of his Representative and Surety, Jesus Christ (Romans 10:3-9). Justification is not the forgiveness of a man without righteousness, but a declaration that he possesses a righteousness which perfectly and forever satisfies the law, namely, Christ's righteousness (2 Corinthians 5:21; Romans 4:6-8).

The sole condition on which this righteousness is imputed or credited to the believer is faith in or on the Lord Jesus Christ. Faith is called a "condition," not because it possesses any merit, but only because it is the instrument, the only instrument by which the soul appropriates or apprehends Christ and his righteousness (Romans 1:17; 3:25, 26; 4:20, 22; Philippians 3:8-11; Galatians 2:16).

The act of faith which thus secures our justification secures also at the same time our sanctification; and thus the doctrine of justification by faith does not lead to licentiousness (Romans 6:2-7). Good works, while not the ground, are the certain consequence of justification (Romans 6:14; 7:6).

Post Apostolic Christians believe that justification by faith alone is one of the chief goals of Scripture, and that any and every other view of

Session 8: *Salvation*

justification serves only to condemn the believer. They believe that Christianity is absolutely integral with the central message of Genesis, which continues and never changes throughout Scripture. That message is that Abraham was justified, accounted as righteous by God, by his faith. This was in advance of the crucifixion, which was to make saving faith possible. After the crucifixion and resurrection, Paul was able to write: 'What does the Scripture say? "Abraham believed God, and it was credited (i.e. imputed) to him as righteousness."' Evangelicals believe that mankind can be accounted righteous before God, but by one means only, which is faith.

It is not possible to mix works with faith in the context of justification. As soon as one believes that one needs, or can do good works to earn justification, one loses saving faith. That is because of what one puts faith in, the atoning work of a perfect sacrifice, i.e. Christ's death on the cross. By deeming works necessary we deem Christ imperfect (see Romans 3:22-25). The term 'faith alone' is theologically unnecessary, and is used only because of the erroneous beliefs of those who think that faith can be augmented with works in order to justify.

No sacrament or any church ritual is at all relevant in this matter; full justification takes place at the moment a sinner admits sin and trusts in the sacrifice of Christ who took the punishment for that sin. Sanctification is what follows as a result of gratitude for justification already completed; it must never be confused with justification. Justification is the precursor, pre-requisite and efficient cause of sanctification. The author of Hebrews wrote: 'How much more, then, will the blood of Christ, who through the eternal Spirit offered himself unblemished to God, purify our consciences from acts that lead to death, so that we may serve the living God!' (Hebrews 9:14). The approach of some is that good works are in some way meritorious. They are not; they are mankind's duty (see Micah 6:8 and Luke 17:7-10). In this context there is no such thing as a good work.

Session 8: *Salvation*

No one can be saved by works, because just one sin is sufficient to exclude a person from God's presence and send him or her to everlasting punishment for sin. 'Whoever keeps the whole law but stumbles at just one point is guilty of breaking all of it' (James 2:10). The only truly righteous acts that exist are those done by faith: 'All of us have become like one who is unclean, and all our 'righteous' acts are as filthy clothes' (Isaiah 64:6). For the believer, 'everything that does not come from faith is sin'. (Romans 14:23)

All of a person's sins must be treated as having never been committed if God is to accept him or her. No amount of good works can ever compensate. God in Christ provided a solution by sacrifice of Himself for the sins of the whole world. Those who believe that He did this, and behave with gratitude for his sacrifice, are accounted righteous; that is, justified by God. Those who do not accept Christ's sacrifice, because they do not believe that they are sinners deserving punishment, or because they do not wish to live lives of gratitude for His sacrifice, are condemned because they refuse Christ's offer of salvation. Mere head belief that Christ died to pay for sins is not faith that justifies. It was that nominal faith that James referred to in his letter (chapter 2), not real faith, which would not have earned James' rebuke.

The justified soul can say with Paul, 'not having a righteousness of my own that comes from keeping the law by works, but that which is through faith in Christ' (Philippians 3:9).

The Post Apostolic Christian (P.A.C.) believes that justification is a singular act in which God declares an unrighteous individual to be righteous because of the work of Jesus. Justification is granted to all who have faith, but even that is viewed as a gift from God (Ephesians 2:8). Justification is seen as being one of the foundational theological fault lines that divided Roman Catholic from the Protestant during the Reformation.

Session 8: *Salvation*

Preservation

Perseverance of the Saints is the name that is used to summarize what the Bible teaches about the eternal security of the believer. It answers the question: Once a person is saved, can they lose their salvation? Perseverance of the saints is the P in the acronym TULIP, which is commonly used to enumerate what are known as the five points of Calvinism. Because the name perseverance of the saints can cause people to have the wrong idea about what is meant, some people prefer to use terms like: "Preservation of the Saints," "Eternal Security," or "Held by God." Each of these terms reveals some aspect of what the Bible teaches about the security of the believer. However like any biblical doctrine what is important is not the name assigned to the doctrine but how accurately it summarizes what the Bible teaches about that subject. No matter which name you use to refer to this important doctrine a thorough study of the Bible will reveal that when it is properly understood it is an accurate description of what the Bible teaches.

The simplest explanation of this doctrine is the saying: "Once saved, always saved." The Bible teaches that those who are born-again will continue trusting in Christ forever. God, by His own power through the indwelling presence of the Holy Spirit, keeps or preserves the believer forever. This wonderful truth is seen in Ephesians 1:13-14 where we see that believers are "sealed with the Holy Spirit of promise, who is the guarantee of our inheritance until the redemption of the purchase possession, to the praise of His glory." When we are born again, we receive the promised indwelling presence of the Holy Spirit that is God's guarantee that He who began a good work in us will complete it (Philippians 1:6). In order for us to lose our salvation after receiving the promised Holy Spirit, God would have to break His promise or renege on His "guarantee," which He cannot do. Therefore the believer is eternally secure because God is eternally faithful.

Session 8: *Salvation*

The understanding of this doctrine really comes from understanding the unique and special love that God has for His children. Romans 8:28-39 tells us that 1) no one can bring a charge against God's elect; 2) nothing can separate the elect from the love of Christ; 3) God makes everything work together for the good of the elect; and 4) all whom God saves will be glorified. God loves His children (the elect) so much that nothing can separate them from Him. Of course this same truth is seen in many other passages of Scripture as well. In John 10:27-30 Jesus says: "My sheep hear My voice, and I know them, and they follow Me; and I give eternal life to them, and they will never perish; and no one will snatch them out of My hand. My Father, who has given them to Me, is greater than all; and no one is able to snatch them out of the Father's hand. I and the Father are one." Again in John 6:37-47 we see Jesus stating that everyone that the Father gives to the Son will come to Him and He will raise all of them up at the last day.

Another evidence from Scripture of eternal security of a believer is found in verses like John 5:24 where Jesus says: "Truly, truly, I say to you, he who hears My word, and believes Him who sent Me, has eternal life, and does not come into judgment, but has passed out of death into life." Notice that eternal life is not something we get in the future but is something that we have once we believe. By its very nature eternal life must last forever or it could not be eternal. This passage says that if we believe the Gospel we have eternal life and will not come into judgment, therefore it can be said we are eternally secure.

There is really very little scriptural basis that can be used to argue against the eternal security of the believer. While there are a few verses that, if not considered in their context, might give the impression that one could "fall from grace" or lose their salvation, when these verses are carefully considered in context it is clear that is not the case. Many people know someone who at one time expressed faith in Christ and who might have appeared to be a genuine Christian who later departed from the faith and now wants to have nothing to do with Christ or His church. These people might even deny the very existence of God. For those that do not want to accept what the Bible

Session 8: *Salvation*

says about the security of the believer these types of people are proof that the doctrine of eternal security cannot be right. However, the Bible indicates otherwise and it teaches that people such as those who profess Christ as Savior at one time only to later walk away and deny Christ, were never truly saved in the first place. For example 1 John 2:19 says, "They went out from us, but they were not of us; for if they had been of us, they would have remained with us; but they went out from us, in order that it might be made manifest that they all are not truly of us." The Bible is also clear that not everyone who professes to be a Christian truly is. Jesus Himself says that not everyone who says "Lord, Lord" will enter the kingdom of heaven (Matthew 7:21-22). Rather than proving we can lose our salvation, those people who profess Christ and fall away simply reinforces the importance of testing our salvation to make sure we are in the faith (2 Corinthians 13:5) and making our calling and election sure by continually examining our lives to make sure we are growing in godliness (2 Peter 1:10).

One of the misconceptions about the doctrine of the perseverance of the saints is that it will lead to "carnal Christians" who believe that since they are eternally secure they can live whatever licentious lifestyle they wish and still be saved. But that is a misunderstanding of the doctrine and what the Bible teaches. A person who believes they can live any way they want because they have professed Christ is not demonstrating true saving faith (1 John 2:3-4). Our eternal security rests on the biblical teaching that those whom God justifies, He will also glorify (Romans 8:29-30). Those who are saved will indeed be conformed to the image of Christ through the process of sanctification (1 Corinthians 6:11). When a person is saved, the Holy Spirit breaks the bondage of sin and gives the believer a new heart and a desire to seek holiness. Therefore a true Christian will desire to be obedient to God and will be convicted by the Holy Spirit when they sin. They will never "live any way they want" because such behavior is impossible for someone who has been given a new nature (2 Corinthians 5:17).

Session 8: *Salvation*

Clearly the doctrine of the perseverance of the saints does accurately represent what the Bible teaches on this important subject. If someone is truly saved, they have been made alive by the Holy Spirit and have a new heart with new desires. There is no way that one that has been "born again" can later be unborn. Because of His unique love for His children, God will keep all of His children safe from harm and Jesus has promised that He would lose none of His sheep. The doctrine of the perseverance of the saints recognizes that true Christians will always persevere and are eternally secure because God keeps them that way. It is based on the fact that Jesus, the "author and perfecter of faith" (Hebrews 12:2), is able to completely save those that the Father has given Him (Hebrews 7:25) and to keep them saved through all eternity.

The following outline on Preservation is © Copyright 1996-2011 by John H. Stoll:

The basis of this doctrine is found in Romans 8. A definition of this truth: Once an individual has willfully accepted the regenerating work of Christ, and is justified (i.e. declared righteous by God), it is impossible for God's child to become an eternally lost person. In John 10:27, Christ says of His own, "... I know them." This is the Greek present tense, which never ends.

There are five Biblical principles that undergird this doctrine:

I. God's Preservation of the Christian is Based on the Perfection of Christ's One Offering on the Cross - Hebrews 10:10-14.

    1. The book of Hebrews contrasts the many sacrifices offered under the law, with the one sacrifice of Christ.

        a. Under the Old Covenant (i.e. Old Testament), a new sacrifice was offered for every sin, because the previous sacrifice could not atone for the present sin. Hebrews 10:11.

Session 8: *Salvation*

    b. In Romans 3:25-26 there is the O.T. manner of Justification (v.25) and the N.T. manner (v.26). In the O.T. God ordained animal sacrifice as a temporary measure, through faith, awaiting the fulfillment of a promised redeemer in the future who would forever pay for sin. In the N.T. way of Justification (v.26), God is now able to declare righteous the believing sinner based on the ground of Christ's one offering on the cross (Hebrews 10:10).

2. In Hebrews 10:10-14 there is the O.T. way contrasted with the N.T. way, showing the superiority of Christ's once for all sacrifice, which was accepted by God for every believer (Hebrews 10:12).

    a. The sacrifice of Christ is perfect forever, for each child of God. Reason: Because His sacrifice is forever and continuously accepted by God in our behalf. The sacrifice is not dependent upon the person, but the person upon the sacrifice.

    b. In Hebrews 9:11-12,23, Christ, as our High Priest offered Himself, once in our behalf, forever. If we deny His eternal sacrifice for us, we put a slight on the perfect, finished work of Christ, and relegate it to the level of the offerings of bulls and goats in the O.T. Why? Because if we say that the blood of Christ is insufficient for us to be eternally saved, then Christ's work was not perfect, and He will have to die again for us.

3. Many are afraid this doctrine will lead people to be careless about their spiritual lives, therefore they stress the other side, i.e. good works to retain one's eternal life. But, they do not see that this is a practical denial of Christ's finished and completed work. One is eternally saved because the work of Christ abides eternally. Salvation is not one holding on to God, but a declaration of God's righteousness keeping one eternally saved, by His holding on to us.

Session 8: *Salvation*

II. The Preservation of the Believer is Based Upon the Resurrection of Christ from the Grave: 1 Corinthians 15:3-4.

> 1. Like as Christ was buried in death, taking with Him our sins, so the Christian who accepts His completed work is dead to the power of sin, and because He arose from the grave, the Christian is alive to resurrection life, as a new creation in Christ Jesus. This gives to the believer eternal life in Christ (Colossians 2:12). Thus, one has resurrection life with Christ, which is eternal as He is eternal, and as incapable of dissolution or death, as Christ is incapable of dissolution or death.
>
> 2. Also, by union with the resurrected Christ, through the baptism of the Holy Spirit (i.e. the operation of the H.S. placing one into the family of God - See 1 Corinthians 12:13), and the impartation of His eternal life, the Christian is made part of the new creation with Christ. Since Christ cannot fall/fail, there is no possibility for even the weakest Christian to fall/fail, who is in Him (Ephesians 1:7; 1 Peter 1:5).

III. The Preservation of the Believer is Based on the Perseverance and Omnipotent Power of the Holy Spirit.

> 1. By the regenerating power of the Holy Spirit the believer is made a child of God (Romans 8:16). Having thus been born of God, the Christian has partaken of the divine nature (1 Peter 1:23; 2 Peter 1:4), and that nature is never said to be removed.
>
> 2. By the fact that the Holy Spirit now indwells every believer and never leaves that person (John 14:16). As a child of God one may grieve the Holy Spirit by unconfessed sin (Ephesians 4:30), but His presence is never said to be removed from one's life.
>
> 3. By the Holy Spirit's ministry in baptizing, the believer is joined to that body of which Christ is the head. (Galatians 3:27). Thus the believer is "In Christ", and in that union old things are passed away and all positions and relationships have become new and are in God (2 Corinthians 5:17). Being accepted forever in God's family, the child of God is as secure as the one to whom he is related is eternal, and in whom he stands.

Session 8: *Salvation*

4. By the fact that God's Word declares that all Christians are sealed with the Holy Spirit unto the day of Redemption (Ephesians 1:13; 4:30).

   a. "Sealed" means a "finished transaction", and in Philippians 1:6, the Apostle Paul noted, "I am confident of this very thing, that the Holy Spirit who has begun a good work in you through regeneration will perform it completely unto the day of Jesus Christ". In other words he is stating that when we were poor sinners, the Holy Spirit had sufficient power to break down our opposition to God, and bring to an end our unbelief and rebellion, do we think for one moment that He does not have enough power to subdue our will as a believer, and carry on to completion the work he has begun?

   b. The reason a Christian continues to the end, is not because of any particular perseverance of his own, but that of the Holy Spirit. When the Holy Spirit begins a work in the heart of a believer, He never gives up until it is completed. This is our confidence.

IV. The Preservation of the Believer is Based Upon the Fact of the New Creation – 2 Corinthians 5:14-17.

   1. Being born again signifies the Christian is of a new creation (i.e. spiritual, not physical).

      a. When we were born into this world, we were members of the original Adamic creation, who was the Father of us all. This creation was not by any act of our own.

      b. When by our own volition of accepting Christ, we become a new creation in Him (i.e. spiritual). See: 2 Corinthians 5:17.

   2. Adam was created sinless, but he fell into sin. Christ came, the sinless one to raise up sinful, fallen mankind.

      a. As at one time we were partakers of Adam's race, now we are made partakers of a new creation, "In Christ".

Session 8: *Salvation*

b. What does God do for us now? Does He put us where Adam was before and say, "Now behave yourself and you will not die again?" No, He puts us up higher than Adam could have ever gone, except by a new and divine creation (Ephesians 2:6). Thus, because we belong to His new creation we can never be an eternally lost soul.

3. Mankind was originally lost because the head of the old creation Adam, failed, and mankind went down with him.

a. As Christians we can never be lost, unless Christ, the head of the new creation falls, and if He does, then the Christian will go down with Him.

b. Thanks be to God, Christ remains a living token of complete satisfaction to God in His work for us, and thus we never will fail or fall, for He will never fall. See: Hebrews 7:25.

V. The Christian's Preservation is Based Upon the Fact That the Believer is the Present Possessor of Eternal Life – John 10:27-28

1. Adam's life was a forfeitable life; he lost it because of sin. Eternal life is non-forfeitable life, otherwise it would not be eternal.

a. In John 3:15-16 eternal life is mentioned, which in the Greek is the present tense, meaning eternal life, now. Furthermore, the present tense is an ongoing infinite element, meaning that eternal life will never run out. It is ad infinitum, eternally.

b. In John 3:36 it says, "He that believes on the Son, has (present tense) everlasting life".

c. Again, John 5:24, uses the word "has", the same as in John 3:36, but adds, "... and shall not come into judgment, but is passed from death unto life". The latter part of the phrase is in the present tense, meaning, NOW.

Session 8: *Salvation*

      d. Therefore, the believer in Christ is already the possessor of eternal life, and is now passed from death unto eternal life.

2. In John 10:27-28 we have the strongest passage for the eternal preservation of the Christian.

      a. Christ is stating that He calls His sheep (i.e. Christians), and they follow Him (v.27).

      b. Then (v.28) He says, "I give unto them eternal life, and they shall never perish, neither shall anyone pluck them out of my hand". The word "perish" should be better translated, "destroy themselves". In the Greek this word is in the subjunctive mood, which lends itself to the stronger translation.

      c. Thus, there is in this verse God's answer to the two objections to eternal, non-forfeitable life, i.e. 1) either God will take eternal life away from you, or, 2) you can take yourself out of His hand. The Christian can never destroy himself, nor can anyone take eternal life from him; it is guaranteed by the omnipotent power of God Himself.

VI. Conclusion: It does not matter what profession a person may make, if one does not accept God's offer of eternal life, through faith and commitment to Christ's work on the cross, that individual is not a regenerated person. That one may be as those of whom Peter speaks in 2 Peter 2:20-22, "But it is happened unto them according to the true proverb, The dog is turned to his own vomit again; and the sow that was washed to her wallowing in the mire". It is one thing to "whitewash" the pig on the outward appearance, it is quite another matter to change the very nature of the pig. A profession without possession is like a whitewash, whereas regeneration in Christ changes a life.

Propitiation

Propitiation (*hilasterion*) is the sacrifice of Jesus Christ that satisfies the just demands of God's holy Law on the believing sinner so God can forgive him and turn away His wrath.

Hilasterion is used as a "propitiatory sacrifice" ("sacrifice of atonement" (NIV), or "propitiation" in Romans 3:25." In Hebrews 9:5, the same Greek word is translated "mercy seat," (NASB) or "propitiatory place" ("the place of atonement" (NIV).

God gave His Son as the means of propitiation for our sins (1 John 2:2; 4:10). A holy God required atonement for sin and provided the perfect sacrifice.

A word of caution is called for because the New Testament does not include the idea of a pagan offering a sacrifice as a means of appeasing the anger and displeasure of his gods.

In the New Testament it is the LORD God who is propitiated by the vindication of His holy character through His own provision that He has made in the vicarious sacrifice of His Son Jesus Christ. Based upon the death of Christ, God can now show His mercy to the believing sinner. The barrier that sin interposed between God and man is broken down and removed. Christ by His death annulled the power of sin to separate God and the believer.

Jesus Christ is the (*hilasmos*) in that He became the sacrifice which perfectly met the demands of the broken law. According to the New Testament usage, (*hilasmos*) is not that of placating the anger of a vengeful God, but the satisfying of His righteousness so that His character and government might be maintained, and at the same time His mercy might be shown to the believer in Jesus Christ.

Session 8: *Salvation*

The Scriptural background for the idea is found in the Jewish Day of Atonement and the sprinkling of sacrificial blood to cover or atone for Israel's sin (Leviticus 16.15), and thus satisfy a holy God for another year. In the New Testament, Jesus' death is viewed as the final sacrifice which completely satisfies God's demands against sinners, and the turning away the wrath of God from all who believe on Jesus Christ.

Jesus Christ is God's propitiatory sacrifice for sin. Jesus had to die on the cross in order to satisfy the Law and justify lost sinners. Jesus suffered the wrath of God on the cross for the sins of the world and fully met the just demands of God's Law.

The Ark of the Covenant contained the testimony of God which consisted of the tables of stone upon which were written the Ten Commandments, a piece of manna and the budded rod of Aaron. The high priest went into the Holy of Holies on the Day of Atonement and sprinkled the sacrificial blood on the golden cover or lid on top of the

Ark of the Covenant. When the blood of the sacrificial victim was sprinkled on this Mercy Seat, it ceased to be a place of judgment and became the place of mercy. The blood came between the violated Law of God and the people who violated it. The Old Testament rite is a beautiful picture of the blood of Jesus Christ, the Lamb of God that satisfies the just requirements of God's law, and paid the penalty of the sinner in full.

There is no denying the fact that "the wages of sin is death" (Romans 6:23). However, the New Testament teaching on the propitiation is far removed from the pagan idea which appeased the anger of the gods because the broken Law of God has been satisfied by Jesus Christ. "And He Himself is the propitiation for our sins; and not for ours only, but also for those of the whole world" (1 John 2:2). "In this is love,

Session 8: *Salvation*

not that we loved God, but that He loved us and sent His Son to be the propitiation for our sins" (1 John 4:10). It is true the Law demanded of every person perfect obedience or death (Romans 6:23; Ezek. 18:4). But Jesus Christ is both the Mercy Seat and the perfect sacrifice which transforms the judgment seat into the throne of mercy. Our salvation is free, but definitely is not cheap. It came at a tremendous cost to God. G. Campbell Morgan said wisely, "It doesn't cost me anything to be saved, but it cost God the life of His Son."

The saving work of Jesus Christ is appropriated "through faith in His blood" (Romans 3:22, 25). "Even the righteousness of God through faith in Jesus Christ for all those who believe; for there is no distinction… whom God displayed publicly as a propitiation in His blood through faith. This was to demonstrate His righteousness, because in the forbearance of God He passed over the sins previously committed" (Romans 3:22, 25).

By the death and shedding of the blood of Jesus Christ the penalty for our sins has been paid in full, and the righteousness of God has been satisfied. The wrath of God has been propitiated; that is appeased and turned aside. The believer places his or her faith in Jesus Christ and God counts it as righteousness. "Much more then, having now been justified by His blood, we shall be saved from the wrath of God through Him" (Romans 5:9).

How could a holy God "be just and at the same time justify the ungodly?" The LORD God must be consistent with His own righteousness and the just demands of His own Law against all sinners, and at the same time demonstrate His grace, love and tender mercy. Both needs are perfectly met in the propitiatory sacrifice of Jesus Christ.

Session 8: *Salvation*

Reconciliation

We are naturally children of wrath (Ephesians 2:3), and are at enmity with God (Ephesians 2:11-15); but, "...we were reconciled to God through the death of His Son..." (Romans 5:10). Because of the death of Jesus, the Christian's relationship with God is changed for the better. Our reconciliation with God is not the result of our own efforts or performance; it is exclusively the result of God's work in Christ. We are now able to have fellowship with Him (1 John 1:3) whereas before we could not. So, we are reconciled to Him (Romans 5:10-11). The problem of sin that separates us from God (Isaiah 59:2) has been addressed and removed in the cross. It was accomplished by God in Christ (2 Corinthians 5:18).

Reconciliation comes from the Greek family of words that has its roots in *allasso*. The meaning common to this word group is "change" or "exchange." Reconciliation involves a change in the relationship between God and man or man and man. It assumes there has been a breakdown in the relationship, but now there has been a change from a state of enmity and fragmentation to one of harmony and fellowship. In Romans 5:6-11, Paul says that before reconciliation we were powerless, ungodly, sinners, and enemies; we were under God's wrath (v. 9). Because of a changed relationship, or reconciliation, we went from being an enemy to God to being God's friend.

Reconciliation has to do with the relationships between God and man. God reconciles the world to himself (2 Corinthians 5:18). Reconciliation takes place through the cross of Christ or the death of Christ. Second Corinthians 5:18 says that "God reconciled us to himself through Christ." God reconciles us to himself through the death of his Son (Romans 5:1). Thus, we are no longer enemies, ungodly, sinners, or powerless. Instead, the love of God has been poured out in our hearts through the Holy Spirit whom he has given to us (Romans 5:5). It is a change in the total state of our lives. The whole message of reconciliation is centered around the love of God and the death of Christ. Paul reminds us that "God demonstrates his own love for us in this: While we were still sinners, Christ died for us" (Romans 5:8). This brings peace with God, access to God through Christ, rejoicing in the hope of the glory of God, making us rejoice in suffering, and having the love of God poured out in our hearts through the Holy Spirit (Romans 5:1-5). We rejoice in God through our Lord Jesus Christ, through whom we have now received reconciliation (Romans 5:11).

Session 8: *Salvation*

Redemption

Redemption is the purchase back of something that had been lost, by the payment of a ransom. The Greek word so rendered is *apolutrosis*, a word occurring nine times in Scripture, and always with the idea of a ransom or price paid, i.e., redemption by a *lutron* (see Matthew 20:28; Mark 10:45). There are instances in the LXX. Version of the Old Testament of the use of *lutron* in man's relation to man (Leviticus 19:20; 25:51; Exodus 21:30; Numbers 35:31, 32; Isaiah 45:13; Proverbs 6:35), and in the same sense of man's relation to God (Numbers 3:49; 18:15).

There are many passages in the New Testament which represent Christ's sufferings under the idea of a ransom or price, and the result thereby secured is a purchase or redemption (comp. Acts 20:28; 1 Corinthians 6:19, 20; Galatians 3:13; 4:4, 5; Ephesians 1:7; Colossians 1:14; 1 Timothy 2:5, 6; Titus 2:14; Hebrews 9:12; 1 Peter 1:18, 19; Revelation 5:9). The idea running through all these texts, however various their reference, is that of payment made for our redemption. The debt against us is not viewed as simply cancelled, but is fully paid. Christ's blood or life, which he surrendered for them, is the "ransom" by which the deliverance of his people from the servitude of sin and from its penal consequences is secured. It is the plain doctrine of Scripture that "Christ saves us neither by the mere exercise of power, nor by his doctrine, nor by his example, nor by the moral influence which he exerted, nor by any subjective influence on his people, whether natural or mystical, but as a satisfaction to divine justice, as an expiation for sin, and as a ransom from the curse and authority of the law, thus reconciling us to God by making it consistent with his perfection to exercise mercy toward sinners" (Hodge's Systematic Theology).

Regeneration

Regeneration is the spiritual change wrought in the heart of man by the Holy Spirit in which his/her inherently sinful nature is changed so that

Session 8: *Salvation*

he/she can respond to God in Faith, and live in accordance with His Will (Matthew 19:28; John 3:3,5,7; Titus 3:5). It extends to the whole nature of man, altering his governing disposition, illuminating his mind, freeing his will, and renewing his nature.

Regeneration, or new birth, is an inner re-creating of fallen human nature by the gracious sovereign action of the Holy Spirit (John 3:5-8). The Bible conceives salvation as the redemptive renewal of man on the basis of a restored relationship with God in Christ, and presents it as involving "a radical and complete transformation wrought in the soul (Romans 12:2; Ephesians 4:23) by God the Holy Spirit (Titus 3:5; Eph. 4:24), by virtue of which we become 'new men' (Ephesians 4:24; Colossians 3:10), no longer conformed to this world (Romans 12:2; Ephesians 4:22; Colossians 3:9), but in knowledge and holiness of the truth created after the image of God (Ephesians 4:24; Colossians 3:10; Romans 12:2)" (B. B. Warfield, Biblical and Theological Studies, 351). Regeneration is the "birth" by which this work of new creation is begun, as sanctification is the "growth" whereby it continues (1 Peter 2:2; 2 Peter 3:18). Regeneration in Christ changes the disposition from lawless, Godless self-seeking (Romans 3:9-18; 8:7) which dominates man in Adam into one of trust and love, of repentance for past rebelliousness and unbelief, and loving compliance with God's law henceforth. It enlightens the blinded mind to discern spiritual realities (1 Corinthians 2:14-15; 2 Corinthians 4:6; Colossians 3:10), and liberates and energizes the enslaved will for free obedience to God (Romans 6:14, 17-22; Philippians 2:13).

The use of the figure of new birth to describe this change emphasizes two facts about it. The first is its decisiveness. The regenerate man has forever ceased to be the man he was; his old life is over and a new life has begun; he is a new creature in Christ, buried with him out of reach of condemnation and raised with him into a new life of righteousness (see Romans 6:3-11; 2 Corinthians 5:17; Colossians 3:9-11). The second fact emphasized is the monergism of regeneration. Infants do not induce, or cooperate in, their own procreation and birth; no more can those who are "dead in trespasses and sins" prompt the quickening operation of God's Spirit within them (see Ephesians 2:1-10). Spiritual

Session 8: *Salvation*

vivification is a free, and to man mysterious, exercise of divine power (John 3:8), not explicable in terms of the combination or cultivation of existing human resources (John 3:6), not caused or induced by any human efforts (John 1:12-13) or merits (Titus 3:3-7), and not, therefore, to be equated with, or attributed to, any of the experiences, decisions, and acts to which it gives rise and by which it may be known to have taken place.

The noun "regeneration" (*palingenesia*) occurs only twice. In Matthew 19:28 it denotes the eschatological "restoration of all things" (Acts 3:21) under the Messiah for which Israel was waiting. This echo of Jewish usage points to the larger scheme of cosmic renewal within which that of individuals finds its place. In Titus 3:5 the word refers to the renewing of the individual. Elsewhere, the thought of regeneration is differently expressed.

In OT prophecies regeneration is depicted as the work of God renovating, circumcising, and softening Israelite hearts, writing his laws upon them, and thereby causing their owners to know, love, and obey him as never before (Deuteronomy 30:6; Jeremiah 31:31-34; 32:39-40; Ezekiel 11:19-20; 36:25-27). It is a sovereign work of purification from sin's defilement (Ezekiel 36:25; cf. Psalms 51:10), wrought by the personal energy of God's creative outbreathing the personal energy of God's creative outbreathing ("spirit": Ezekiel 36:27; 39:29). Jeremiah declares that such renovation on a national scale will introduce and signal God's new messianic administration of his covenant with his people (Jeremiah 31:31; 32:40).

In the NT the thought of regeneration is more fully individualized, and in John's Gospel and First Epistle the figure of new birth, "from above" (anothen: John 3:3, 7, Moffatt), "of water and the Spirit" (i.e., through a purificatory operation of God's Spirit: see Ezekiel 36:25-27; John 3:5; cf. 3:8), or simply "of God" (John 1:13, nine times in 1 John), is integral to the presentation of personal salvation. The verb *gennao* (which means both "beget" and "bear") is used in these passages in the aorist or perfect tense to denote the once-for-all divine work whereby the sinner, who before was only "flesh," and as such,

Session 8: *Salvation*

whether he knew it or not, utterly incompetent in spiritual matters (John 3:3-7), is made "spirit" (John 3:6), i.e., is enabled and caused to receive and respond to the saving revelation of God in Christ. In the Gospel, Christ assures Nicodemus that there are no spiritual activities, no seeing or entering God's kingdom, because no faith in himself, without regeneration (John 3:1ff.); and John declares in the prologue that only the regenerate receive Christ and enter into the privileges of God's children (John 1:12-13). Conversely, in the Epistle John insists that there is no regeneration that does not issue in spiritual activities. The regenerate do righteousness (1 John 2:29) and do not live a life of sin (3:9; 5:18: the present tense indicates habitual law-keeping, not absolute sinlessness, cf. 1:8-10); they love Christians (4:7), believe rightly in Christ, and experience faith's victory over the world (5:4). Any who do otherwise, whatever they claim, are still unregenerate children of the devil (3:6-10).

Paul specifies the Christological dimensions of regeneration by presenting it as (1) a lifegiving coresurrection with Christ (Ephesians 2:5; Colossians 2:13; cf. 1 Peter 1:3); (2) a work of new creation in Christ (2 Corinthians 5:17; Ephesians 2:10; Galatians 6:15). Peter and James make the further point that God "begets anew" (*anagennao*: 1 Peter 1:23) and "brings to birth" (*apokyeo*: James 1:18) by means of the gospel. It is under the impact of the word that God renews the heart, so evoking faith (Acts 16:14-15).

Historical Discussion: The fathers did not formulate the concept of regeneration precisely. They equated it, broadly speaking, with baptismal grace, which to them meant primarily (to Pelagius, exclusively) remission of sins. Augustine realized, and vindicated against Pelagianism, the necessity for prevenient grace to make man trust and love God, but he did not precisely equate this grace with regeneration. The Reformers reaffirmed the substance of Augustine's doctrine of prevenient grace, and Reformed theology still maintains it. Calvin used the term "regeneration" to cover man's whole subjective renewal, including conversion and sanctification. Many seventeenth century Reformed theologians equated regeneration with effectual calling and conversion with regeneration (hence the systematic mistranslation of *epistrepho*, "turn," as a passive, "be converted," in the AV); later Reformed theology has defined regeneration more narrowly, as the implanting of the "seed" from which faith and repentance spring (1 John 3:9) in the course of effectual calling. Arminianism constructed the doctrine of regeneration synergistically, making man's renewal dependent on his prior cooperation with grace; liberalism constructed it naturalistically, identifying regeneration with a moral change or a religious experience. The fathers lost the biblical understanding of the ordinances as symbolic representations of spiritual truths, and replaced them with sacraments to stir up faith and seals to confirm believers in possession of the blessings signified, and so came to regard baptism as conveying the regeneration which they believed it signified (Titus 3:5) ex opere operato to those who did not obstruct it's working. Since infants could not do this, all baptized infants were accordingly held to be regenerated. This view has persisted in all the non-Reformed churches of Christendom, and among sacramentalists within Protestantism.

Repentance

The Greek word *metanoeo*, is translated as repentance that expresses the true New Testament idea of the spiritual change implied in a sinner's return to God. The term signifies "to have another mind," to change the opinion or purpose with regard to sin. It is equivalent to the Old Testament word "turn." Thus, it is employed by John the Baptist, Jesus, and the apostles (Matthew 3:2; Mark 1:15; Acts 2:38). The idea expressed by the word is intimately associated with different aspects of spiritual transformation and of Christian life, with the process in which the agency of man is prominent, as faith (Acts 20:21), and as conversion (Acts 3:19); also with those experiences and blessings of which God alone is the author, as remission and forgiveness of sin (Luke 24:47; Acts 5:31). As a vital experience, repentance is to manifest its reality by producing good fruits appropriate to the new spiritual life (Matthew 3:8). The believer is given by God a changed mind; a renewed mind of Christ that transforms the believer into the image of Christ (Romans 8:5-7; 12:1-2).

Session 8: *Salvation*

Repentance is necessary for salvation and means "a change of mind." Dr. C.I. Scofield, in the Scofield Reference Bible (copyrighted in 1909), has the following footnote, "Repentance is the translation of a Greek word (*metanoia/metanoeo*) meaning "to have another mind," "to change the mind," and is used in the New Testament to indicate a change of mind in respect of sin, of God and of self. This change of mind may, especially in the case of Christians who have fallen into sin, be preceded by sorrow (2 Corinthians 7:8-11), but sorrow for sin, though it may "work" repentance, is not repentance. The son in Matthew 21:28-29 illustrate true repentance. Saving faith includes and implies that change of mind, which is called repentance."

There is great difficulty in expressing the true idea of a change of thought with reference to sin when we translate the New Testament "repentance" into other languages. The Latin version renders it "exercise penitence" (poenitentiam agere). But "penitence" etymologically signifies pain, grief, distress, rather than a change of thought and purpose. Thus Latin Christianity has been corrupted by the pernicious error of presenting grief over sin rather than abandonment of sin as the primary idea of New Testament repentance. It was easy to make the transition from penitence to penance, consequently the Romanists represent Jesus and the apostles as urging people to do penance (poenitentiam agite). The English word "repent" is derived from the Latin repoenitere, and inherits the fault of the Latin, making grief the principal idea and keeping it in the background, if not altogether out of sight, the fundamental New Testament conception of a change of mind with reference to sin. Penance is payment for sin. Penitence is sorrow for sin. Works and something of self is turning from sin. But repentance (*metanoia*) means a change of mind. Repentance in salvation means a change of mind from any idea of religion that man might have and accepting God's way of salvation. But the exhortations of the ancient prophets, of Jesus, and of the apostles show that the change of mind is the dominant idea of the words employed, while the accompanying grief and consequent reformation enter into one's experience from the very nature of the case.

Session 8: *Salvation*

Sanctification

Sanctification involves more than a mere moral reformation of character, brought about by the power of the truth: it is the work of the Holy Spirit bringing the whole nature more and more under the influences of the new gracious principles implanted in the soul in regeneration. In other words, sanctification is the carrying on to perfection the work begun in regeneration, and it extends to the whole man (Romans 6:13; 2 Corinthians 4:6; Colossians 3:10; 1 John 4:7; 1 Corinthians 6:19). It is the special office of the Holy Spirit in the plan of redemption to carry on this work (1 Corinthians 6:11; 2 Thessalonians 2:13). Faith is instrumental in securing sanctification, inasmuch as it (1) secures union to Christ (Galatians 2:20), and (2) brings the believer into living contact with the truth, whereby he is led to yield obedience "to the commands, trembling at the threatenings, and embracing the promises of God for this life and that which is to come."

Perfect sanctification (or often referred to as ultimate sanctification) is not attainable in this life (1 Kings 8:46; Proverbs 20:9; Ecclesiastes 7:20; James 3:2; 1 John 1:8). See Paul's account of himself in Romans 7:14-25; Philippians 3:12-14; and 1 Timothy 1:15; also the confessions of David (Psalms 19:12, 13; 51), of Moses (90:8), of Job (42:5, 6), and of Daniel (9:3-20). "The more holy a man is, the more humble, self-renouncing, self-abhorring, and the more sensitive to every sin he becomes, and the more closely he clings to Christ. The moral imperfections which cling to him he feels to be sins, which he laments and strives to overcome. Believers find that their life is a constant warfare, and they need to take the kingdom of heaven by storm, and watch while they pray. They are always subject to the constant chastisement of their Father's loving hand, which can only be designed to correct their imperfections and to confirm their graces. And it has been notoriously the fact that the best Christians have been those who have been the least prone to claim the attainment of perfection for themselves." (Hodge's Outlines).

Session 8: *Salvation*

Sanctification comes from the verb sanctify. Sanctify originates from the Greek word *hagiazo,* which means to be "separate" or to be "set apart" for a holy work. In the Bible, sanctification generally relates to a sovereign act of God whereby He "sets apart" a person, place, or thing in order that His purposes may be accomplished. In the book of Exodus, God sanctifies a place of worship. "And there I will meet with the children of Israel, and the tabernacle shall be sanctified by My glory," says Exodus 29:43. Even a day can be sanctified as seen in Genesis 2:3 where the seventh day is "set apart" as a holy day of rest. "Then God blessed the seventh day and sanctified it, because in it He rested from all His work which God had created and made."

Similarly, when a person is sanctified he or she is being set apart by God for a specific divine purpose. The very moment we are saved in Christ we are also immediately sanctified and begin the process of being conformed to the image of Christ. As God's children we are "set apart" from that moment to carry out His divine purposes unto eternity. Hebrews 10:14 says, "For by one offering He has perfected forever those who are being sanctified."

Jesus had a lot to say about sanctification in the Book of John, chapter 17. In verse 16 the Lord says, "They are not of the world, even as I am not of the world," and this is before His request: "Sanctify them in the truth: Thy word is truth." Sanctification is a state of separation unto God; all believers enter into this state when they are born of God: "But of Him you are in Christ Jesus, who became for us wisdom from God—and righteousness and sanctification and redemption" (1 Corinthians 1:30). This is a once-for-ever separation, eternally unto God. It is an intricate part of our salvation, our connection with Christ (Hebrews 10:10).

Session 8: *Salvation*

Sanctification also refers to the practical experience of this separation unto God, being the effect of obedience to the Word of God in one's life, and is to be pursued by the believer earnestly (1 Peter 1:15; Hebrews 12:14). Just as the Lord prayed in John 17, it has in view the setting

apart of believers for the purpose for which they are sent into the world: "As Thou didst send Me into the world, even so send I them into the world. And for their sakes I sanctify Myself, that they themselves also may be sanctified in truth" (v. 18, 19). That He set Himself apart for the purpose for which He was sent is both the basis and the condition of our being set apart for that for which we are sent (John 10:36). His sanctification is the pattern of, and the power for, ours. The sending and the sanctifying are inseparable. On this account they are called saints, *hagioi* in the Greek; "sanctified ones." Whereas previously their behavior bore witness to their standing in the world in separation from God, now their behavior should bear witness to their standing before God in separation from the world.

There is one more sense that the word sanctification is referred to in Scripture. Paul prayed in 1 Thessalonians 5:23, "The God of peace Himself sanctify you wholly; and may your spirit and soul and body be preserved entire, without blame at the coming of our Lord Jesus Christ." Paul also wrote in Colossians of "the hope which is laid up for you in the heavens, whereof ye heard before in the word of the truth of the Gospel" (Colossians 1:5). He later speaks of Christ Himself as "the hope of glory" (Colossians 1:27) and then mentions the fact of that hope when he says, "When Christ, who is our Life, shall be manifested, then shall ye also with Him be manifested in glory" (Colossians 3:4). This glorified state will be our ultimate separation from sin, total sanctification in every aspect. "Beloved, now we are children of God; and it has not yet been revealed what we shall be, but we know that when He is revealed, we shall be like Him, for we shall see Him as He is" (1 John 3:2).

Session 8: *Salvation*

Sanctification is a work of the triune God, but is ascribed more particularly to the Holy Spirit in Scripture (Romans 8:11; 15:16; 1 Peter 1:2). It is particularly important in our day, with its emphasis on the necessity of approaching the study of theology anthropologically and its one-sided call to service in the kingdom of God, to stress the fact that God, and not man, is the author of sanctification. Especially in view of the activism that is such a characteristic feature of American religious life, and which glorifies the work of man rather than the grace of God, it is necessary to stress the fact over and over again that sanctification is the fruit of justification, that the former is simply impossible without the latter, and that both are the fruits of the grace of God in the redemption of sinners. Though man is privileged to cooperate with the Spirit of God, he can do this only in virtue of the strength which the Spirit imparts to him from day to day. The spiritual development of man is not a human achievement, but a work of divine grace. Man deserves no credit whatsoever for that which he contributes to it instrumentally. In so far as sanctification takes place in the subconscious life, it is effected by the immediate operation of the Holy Spirit. But as a work in the conscious life of believers it is wrought by several means, which the Holy Spirit employs.

To summarize, sanctification is the same Greek word as holiness, "*hagios*," meaning a separation for a holy work. First, a once-for-all positional separation unto Christ at our salvation. Second, a practical progressive holiness in a believer's life while awaiting the return of Christ. Third, we will be changed into His perfect likeness—holy, sanctified, and completely separated from the presence of evil (i.e. past, progressive, and ultimate sanctification).

Session 8: *Salvation*

notes

Session 9: *The Christian Life*

> **The Christian Life:** a life harmoniously consisting of the Christian faith, doctrine, and practice. The Christian's love for God is expressed through obedience and submission to God's four ordained institutions of authority as stated in the Bible: the authority of the household (1 Corinthians 11:3; Ephesians 5:23; 6:1-4); civil authority (Romans 13:1-7); the authority of scripture (2 Timothy 3:16 – 17; 2 Peter 1:20 – 21; John 10:35 with Matthew 5:18); and the authority of the autonomous functioning church (Ephesians 1:22; 5:23; Colossians 1:18).

1.1 **According to 1 Corinthians 11:3, who is the head of each of the following: Christ; man; and women?**

1.2 **According to Ephesians 5:22, what should wives do and how should they do this? Does this mean they are less important or equal (you may want to refer back to question seven in Session three)?**

1.3 **According to Ephesians 5:25, what should husbands do and how should they do this?**

1.4 **According to Ephesians 6:1-2, what should children do and how should they do this?**

Session 9: *The Christian Life*

2.1 Read Romans 13:1-7 to answer the following questions:

verse 1. How does God want us to interact with governing civil authorities?

verse 1. Who has established or elected the governing civil authorities?

verse 2. If someone rebels against the governing civil authorities, whom are they really rebelling against?

verse 3 and 4. What is the best way not to fear the governing civil authorities?

verse 5. What are at least two reasons why we should obey our governing civil authorities?

verses 6-7. Why should we pay the taxes we owe?

2.2 According to Titus 3:1, what should be our attitude toward our civil authorities?

2.3 According to 1 Timothy 2:1-2, why should we pray for our governing civil authorities?

Session 9: *The Christian Life*

As we have already discussed in Session one that Scripture has come from God. Scripture has been a progressive revelation from God explaining how His people are to live. The Old Testament refers to the Scriptures in a variety of terms. For instance: the Law; statutes; precepts; decrees; commands; ordinances; etc. Though the scriptures were highly respected, people also longed to hear God's Word (i.e. the word of the Lord).

3.1 **List several (at least seven) ways that God spoke in the past ages, eras, or dispensations (note: you may want to refer to question 7 of Session 2).**

3.2 **Read Psalm 19:7-11. What was the purpose of scripture? Does scripture still have this authority and purpose in the Christian's life today?**

3.3 **In our present Church age, what is the only way in which God speaks today (note: you may want to review question 8 in Session one)?**

3.4 **During Jesus' times, there was a distinction between scripture and God's Word (i.e. John 10:35). When do you think Scripture became the sole Word of God for this present Church age?**

Session 9: *The Christian Life*

4.1 According to Matthew 28:18-20, how much authority has been given to the church in order to make disciples?

4.2 According to Matthew 16:18, who do you think can prevent Christ from building His church?

4.3 In Matthew 18:15-20, describe:

verse 15. What should a believer do if another believer sins against them?

verse 16. What should a believer do if their brother or sister who sinned against them does not listen to them?

verse 17. What should a believer do if their brother or sister who sinned against them does not listen to two or three witnesses?

verse 18 and 19. What kind of authority does the church have in the spiritual matters of the church?

verse 20. How many people would you need to operate with the authority of the church?

Session 9: *The Christian Life*

4.4 According to Ephesians 1:22-23 and Colossians 1:18, who is the head or authority of the Church? According to 1 Corinthians 12:12-27, what is the church?

4.5 According to 1 Thessalonians 5:12-13, what should be your attitude toward those who are working hard to instruct you in the Lord? What should your attitude be toward others in the church that are spiritually undisciplined, discouraged, and weak?

4.6 Read 1 Timothy 5:17-20. Why do you think it is so important to not make or entertain an accusation against a mature Christian (unless of course there are two or three witnesses)? Why do you think it is important to *publicly* rebuke those who make or entertain accusations against an elder?

All of the authorities that God has established have specific purposes or functions in a believer's life. The goal for the Christian is to understand God's ordained authorities and learn how to properly interact with them in order to obey and love God. For instance, there are many reasons why people obey the laws of the land. For example, people may stop at a red traffic light so that they will not get a ticket or to insure their safety. Though these are not bad reasons to stop at a red traffic light, the most excellent reason to obey the laws of the land is in order to obey, love, honor, and glorify our heavenly Father.

Session 9: *The Christian Life*

Each God ordained authority has its boundaries based upon the authorities designed purpose. These authorities are not free to contradict or invade another God ordained authority's domain. For example, the governing civil authority does not have the God given right to establish a law prohibiting a believer from praying to God or demanding believers to bow down and worship a false god (e.g. Daniel 3:1-30 and 6:1-28). If the governing civil authority steps outside of their designed boundary and crosses over into another God ordained authority, the Christian should submit to the correct God ordained authority. For example, if a husband instructed his Christian wife to do something that would be immoral, the Christian wife must appeal to and obey the God ordained authority of Scripture and therefore refuse. Or if a boss asked a Christian to lie, the Christian must appeal to and obey the God ordained authority of Scripture, regardless of the consequences.

All of God's ordained authorities have their designed purpose which establishes the boundaries of authority in the Christian's life. The goal of the Christian is to have God's Word dictate these purposes and boundaries in order to be able to submit and obey God in every situation of life. To love God is to obey Him! Submission and obedience to God means being submissive and obedient to: the laws of the land; the authorities of the household; the commands in the Scriptures; and to a functioning autonomous church.

5.0 **Look up John 14:23-24 and 1 John 5:3. How does someone demonstrate that they love God?**

6.0 **According to John 14:21, what will happen if someone has Jesus' commands and obeys them?**

Session 10: *The Church*

> **The Church:** there is one true church, the body and bride of Christ (Ephesians 1:22-23; 5:25-32); composed of all true believers from Pentecost to the return of Christ (1 Corinthians 12:12-27; Acts 2:1-41 with 1 Thessalonians 4:16-17). Present believers are established as functioning churches (1 Corinthians 8:1, 16-24); being autonomous but unified in work and fellowship through doctrine (Ephesians 4:11-16); and each autonomous functioning church being God's ordained institution of authority in the practice of continuing the work of Christ in revealing the Name of God through the Great Commission (John 17:4, 6, 18 and Matthew 28:16-20).

1.0 What physical things of this world does the Bible use to describe the spiritual Church in each of the following?

   a. Ephesians 1:23 with Colossians 1:18 with 1 Corinthians 12:12-27

   b. Ephesians 5:25-32 with John 3:29 with Revelation 19:7

2.0 How do the above biblical descriptions of the church help picture how someone should act toward and within the church?

3.0 According to Ephesians 4:11-13, why did Christ give the early church apostles, prophets, evangelists, shepherds and teachers to the church?

Session 10: *The Church*

There are two common terms used in describing the biblical concept of the Church. One of these terms is the Universal Church. This term is to represent all Christians from the beginning of the Church near two thousand years ago until the Lord's return. The other commonly used term is the local church, which will be called the functioning church from this point forward. The functioning church is exactly that, a group of believers that are operating or functioning together to fulfill the church's purpose as God's ordained authority.

The functioning church is a group of believers that submit to and operate under the authority of God in order to fulfill her purpose. The functioning church is to fulfill the Great Commission by making disciples (Matthew 28:16-20). The functioning church has the authority to excise church discipline and is commanded to observe the ordinances. Each functioning church is autonomous and operates with the full authority of God (i.e. is independent of all other authorities; sovereign; self-governing; self-directed/ruled; self-sufficient).

The functioning church is to continue the ministry of Jesus Christ. The church is His body. He is the head of the Church. The functioning church should reveal Jesus to people so that He in turn will reveal His Father. This brings glory and honor to the Father who in turn will glorify His Son. The very purpose of the church is to glorify God by making disciples.

4.0 **1 Thessalonians 4:16-17 describes Christ returning for His Church. Who composes or makes up the eternal Church (i.e. Universal Church)?**

5.1 **According to John 5:36 who sent Jesus Christ?**

5.2 **According to John 5:36, what was it that testifies to who Jesus is and who it was that sent Him?**

Session 10: *The Church*

6.1 According to John 17:4, did Christ fulfill what the Father sent Him to do?

6.2 According to the above verse, why has He done this?

6.3 According to John 17:6 and 17:26, what has Christ done?

6.4 Summary: Jesus Christ was sent to glorify God by revealing His very essence (i.e. make His name known). Jesus stated that anyone who accepts Him accepts the one who sent Him (i.e. accepts God the Father). Also anyone who accepts anyone that Jesus has sent accepts Jesus and therefore accepts God the Father (John 13:20)! According to John 17:18 how, and for what purpose, has Jesus sent believers into the world?

7.1 According to John 14:12-13, what will someone who has true biblical faith be doing?

7.2 According to the above verses, why do you think Christians will do even greater things than Jesus has done?

7.3 According to the above verses, when we ask Jesus to do things that are in His will (i.e. Jesus' name), why will He do them?

Session 10: *The Church*

8.0 According to Matthew 16:18, who will build the church?

9.0 The purpose of the church is to glorify God by making Him known. The method or way in which the church is to do this is by making disciples. According to Matthew 28:19-20, what are three actions that Christians, as part of a functioning church, are commanded to do in order to make disciples?

10.1 According to Ephesians 5:22-33 with John 3:29:

   a. who is the bride of Christ?

   b. who is head over the church?

   c. why did Christ give Himself up for the church?

   d. how did He cleanse her (also John 15:3)?

10.2 According to Revelation 21:2-3:

   a. what did John see?

   b. how was she prepared?

   c. how was she dressed (Rev. 19:7-8)?

   d. what did John hear the loud voice say?

   e. Read Genesis 17:7; Exodus 6:7; Isaiah 51:16; Jeremiah 11:4; 30:22; 31:33; 32:38; Ezekiel 11:19-20; 14:11; 34:30; 36:28; 37:27-28; Zechariah 8:8; who did God say would be His people?

Session 10: *The Church*

10.3 According to Revelation 21:9-10, 13-14:

a. what did one of the seven angels say he would show John?

b. what did the angel carry John away and show him?

c. how many gates did the city Jerusalem have and what was written above each one?

d. how many foundations did the walls of the city have and what names were written on them?

10.4 According to Hebrews 11:10:

a. Abraham, Isaac, and Jacob, who all lived in tents, were looking forward to what?

b. who is the architect and builder of this city?

10.5 According to Ephesians 2:19-22:

a. who are Christians citizens with?

b. believers are members of what?

c. what is this household built upon?

d. who is the cornerstone of this building?

e. what do Christians rise to become?

f. what are Christians being built together to become?

Session 10: *The Church*

10.6   According to 1 Corinthians 3:16-17, what are believers?

10.7   According to 2 Corinthians 5:1-5:

       a. what kind of house do believers have?

       b. who built this house?

10.8   According to 2 Corinthians 6:16:

       a. who are believers?

       b. who is God referring to when He says, "I will live with *them*..." and "*they* will be my *people*."?

10.9   According to Hebrews 3:6, who are believers?

10.10   According to 1 Peter 2:4-5:

       a. What are believers like?

       b. What are believers being built into?

       c. Why are believers being built into a spiritual house?

10.11   According to Acts 17:24-25:

       a. What kind of temple does God not live in?

       b. Who says they are building what in Matthew 16:18?

10.12   According to 2 Corinthians 5:1, what kind of house do believers have when this earthly tent is destroyed? What kind of hands has not built it?

Session 10: *The Church*

Summary

The church is established and built by Christ in order to continue his earthly ministry. Christ was sent by the Father in order to reveal and thus glorify the Father. We, the church, will desire to do the very things He does. Christ prayed to His Father, "As you have sent me into the world, I have sent them into the world"(John 17:18). Jesus also said to His Father, "I have brought you glory on earth by completing the work you gave me to do... I have revealed you to those you gave me out of the world" (John 17:4, 6). He is the Word (i.e. revealer) of God (John 1:1, Revelation 19:13). He is the exact representation of God (Hebrews 1:3). If you know Christ you know the Father (John 8:19; 14:7, 9). He glorifies the Father by making Him known. This is who Jesus was, is, and will always be. He will always be functioning in this capacity. This is who He is... this is what He does... forever!! And much the same way, this will be how the church will function... forever. We are the New Jerusalem... the House of God... built by Christ... continuing His earthly ministry (i.e. a royal Priesthood)... bringing people to God... bringing Him glory by making Him known... forever and ever and ever. We will be an extension of what our eternal Husband will be doing (i.e. adopting and doing His Will). Israel will be forever coming in and out of the City (i.e. the New Jerusalem) worshipping their God being His people. This is why God delivered them out of Egypt (Exodus 3:18; 4:23; 5:1, 3, etc). He desires to be their God and have them faithfully be His people. They will come to God through Jesus Christ via the Holy Spirit who is living in the very building blocks of the New Jerusalem... the Church! Every tribe of Israel will enter into the New City through their own gate that has been built just for them. Built not by human hands, but by Christ Himself. The way the church is supposed to function in this capacity is by bringing people to Christ so He can glorify the Father by making Him known. The way the church is to fulfill her purpose here on earth is by making disciples of Jesus Christ. And the church will be fulfilling her purpose as the Bride of Christ by being the New Jerusalem for all eternity.

Session 10: *The Church*

notes

Session 11: *The Ordinances*

> **The Ordinances:** the Christian should repeatedly observe the ordinances through and under the authority of the functioning church as commanded by our Lord Jesus Christ, which are: (a). the Upper Room ordinance symbolizing the relationship we have with God through Jesus Christ and consists of, and is to be observed, in the following order: the washing of the saint's feet symbolizing one has already had a cleansing spiritual bath (John 13:1-17); the bread symbolizing the body of Christ (1 Corinthians 11:23-24, 26; 10:16b-17; Hebrews 10:19-22); the cup symbolizing the blood of Christ (1 Corinthians 11:25-26; 10:16a); the Agape Feast symbolizing the fellowship believers have with God and one another (1 Corinthians 11:20-22, 33-34; Jude 12) and (b). the Baptism ordinance: water baptism of disciples of Christ by trine immersion symbolizing the saints identification with the triune God (Matthew 28:19).

The word "ordinance" is not actually found in many of the New Testament English translations of the Bible. Though the actual word ordinance is commonly not in the New Testament, this word does represent a biblical teaching for the church. What the Bible does clearly describe are the commands that are commonly categorized as ordinances.

The biblical commands commonly referred to as ordinances are set apart by the following characteristics:

- *the command was given by Jesus Christ near the end of His earthly ministry*
- *the command entails a specific physical action*
- *the specific physical action has symbolical meaning*
- *the specific physical action that has symbolical meaning, pictures a spiritual reality*
- *the specific physical action with symbolical meaning that pictures a spiritual reality is commanded to be repeatedly performed*
- *the command was given to each individual believer, and is only to be observed through and under the God-ordained institution of the functioning church*

Session 11: *The Ordinances*

1.0 **Fill-in-the-blank:** use the above characteristics to fill in the blank

- *the command was given by _____ _____ near the _____ of His earthly ministry*

- *the command entails a specific _____ action*

- *the specific physical action has _____ meaning*

- *the specific physical action that has symbolical meaning, _____ a spiritual reality*

- *the specific physical action with symbolical meaning that pictures a spiritual reality is commanded to be _____ performed*

- *the command was given to the _____ and is to be repeatedly performed by each individual of the body, but only under and through the authority of the functioning church*

2.0 **From the above definition, what are some reasons why all of Jesus' commands would not be classified as an ordinance?**

There are only two commands found in the Bible that meet all the above characteristics of an ordinance: the Upper Room ordinance (i.e. commonly called the communion service) and the Baptism ordinance.

Session 11: *The Ordinances*

    The Upper Room ordinance is so named because Jesus Christ instituted this ordinance in an upper room of a house. He did this just hours before he would be crucified. He wanted to communicate some vital spiritual truths to these men in a vivid way, which they, or those who came after them, would never forget. Jesus Christ instituted four elements in the following order: the feet washing; the bread; the cup; and the agape feast (commonly called the love feast). It will prove helpful to consider each element individually in order to see the overall picture of the Upper Room ordinance.

The first element of the Upper Room Ordinance: Feet Washing

3.0 Read John 13:6-11 and answer the following questions:

    a. **What condition (clean or unclean) is the individual who only needs to wash his feet (v. 10)?**

    b. **Is he spiritually clean before his feet are washed?**

    c. **What point was Jesus making by only washing Peter's feet, rather than giving his entire body a bath?**

    No one can enter into the Holy presence of God in an unclean state and live (Exodus 33:20). In the Old Testament, only one person once a year would enter into the Holy of Holy places (i.e. where the presence of the glory of God was) to offer an atoning sacrifice for Israel. Before he would enter into the Holy of Holies, he would have to ceremonially be cleansed or he would die. This was a temporary external cleansing. Today, Christians are permanently spiritually cleansed by faith through Jesus Christ! This permanent cleansing that Christ has given to Christians is what feet washing symbolically represents and teaches.

Session 11: *The Ordinances*

The second element of the Upper Room Ordinance: The Bread

4.0 Read and answer the following questions:

a. According to Mark 14:22 what does the bread symbolically represent?

b. A veil or thick curtain separated the glory of God in the Holy of Holies from the Israel people. According to Hebrews 10:19-20, what is the curtain or veil for a Christian?

c. According to Matthew 27:51, what happened to the curtain of Israel's temple at the very moment that Jesus' body expired?

Once a year the High Priest would ceremonially cleanse himself and then pass through the thick curtain or veil that separated the glory of God in the Holy of Holies from the Israelites. God provided this veil as a type of protection for His nation of Israel. If His chosen nation were to be exposed to His glory, they would surely die.

Today, Christ has sufficiently cleansed every Christian. This permanently provides every Christian with 24 hour a day access to the Holy throne of the Almighty! Jesus Christ, that is His body, is the way or path to the Holy throne of God.

Session 11: *The Ordinances*

The third element of the Upper Room Ordinance: The Cup

5.0 Read and answer the following questions:

a. According to Luke 22:20b, what did the grape juice or wine in the cup represent?

b. A covenant is a contract between two people. In this case it is an agreement or contract between man and God. According to Hebrews 9:18, what did it take to put the first covenant (i.e. the covenant between God and Israel) into effect?

c. According to Hebrews 9:22, what does it take for God to forgive sin?

    The child of God has a new and better covenant with the Holy God of the Bible through the blood of Christ than the Israel people of the Old Testament had through their animal sacrifices. Hebrews 7:20b-22 states, "Others became priests without any oath, but he [Jesus Christ] became a priest with an oath when God said to him: 'The Lord has sworn and will not change his mind: 'You are a priest forever.' Because of this oath, Jesus has become the guarantee of a better covenant." The blood of goats and bulls and the ashes of a heifer could only temporarily cover the outward man, but the blood of Christ has permanently cleansed the inward man (Hebrews 9:12-15). Drinking the symbolic blood of The Lamb of God pictures the new covenant we have with God and that this covenant relationship is sealed or secured through Christ blood. His blood is the offered contract of His cleansing, not just the outward part of man, but the very heart and essence of the believer. The Child of God is completely acceptable to God by a new and better covenant than that of Israel.

Session 11: *The Ordinances*

The forth element of the Upper Room Ordinance: The Love Feast:

6.0 Read 1 Corinthians 11:18-34 and answer the following questions:

a. As what were the Corinthian people "coming together" (v.18)?

b. What was the church doing according to verse 21? How does this demonstrate that this "Lord's Supper" or Love Feast was a full meal?

c. The Love Feast symbolically represents the love believers should have towards God and fellow believers. According to John 13:34-35, how did Jesus say people would recognize or know who truly are His disciples?

    The eleven disciples of Christ (Judas had already gone) were present during the Agape Feast and were commanded to love one another (John 13:34-35). Agape is a Greek word for love, so the Agape Feast is a feast of love. The Disciples of Christ were commanded to love one another, and by this love the world would know they are truly disciples of Christ. The kind of love that the disciple of Christ should have for one another is the type of love Christ exhibited for His disciples. Jesus Christ became a servant and laid down his life for His disciples so they could serve (i.e. worship) God. Not only has Christ enabled His Disciples to love one another, but more importantly enabled them to love God.

    Much like the Priests of the old covenant, Christians are a holy priesthood of believers (I Peter 2:5, 9). Like the Priests, we have the opportunity, through the functioning church, to help our brothers and sisters in Christ to worship and obey our God. It is the church, each individual within her, which is to teach one another how to obey all of Christ's commands (Matthew 28:16-20). The Christian church community should encourage, serve, and love one another in order to help the church be a living sacrifice to God. This is our spiritual act of worship (Romans 12:1-4)! This is part of the doctrine known as the Priesthood of the believer.

Session 11: *The Ordinances*

7.0 Match the following elements of the Upper Room ordinance with the correct description of what the element symbolically represents.

____ the Feet Washing

A. Christ's blood was sacrificially, yet willingly shed. His blood provided complete forgiveness so the church can have a new covenant relationship with God.

____ the Bread

B. Because of what Christ has done, we have the most intimate relationship between fellow believers as well as the Holy God of the universe. We serve and glorify God by loving and serving fellow believers. We have an overabundance of love

____ the Cup

C. It is through Jesus Christ's physical body that we have twenty-four hour a day access to God. The veil is opened wide; meaning, we are free to come and go at will.

____ the Agape Feast

D. The church has been completely and permanently spiritually cleansed by a spiritual bath; therefore, believers can approach the Holy throne of God with total confidence.

Session 11: *The Ordinances*

Though there are many different kinds of baptisms in the Bible, in the Baptism ordinance the term "baptism" represents the Christian symbolic water baptism. The word "baptize" simply means to dip, immerse, or saturate as to identify. For example, one could be baptized in fear; which means that they are completely immersed, or identified, in fear. In biblical times, a typical way they would use the term to baptize could be to baptize (i.e. dip or immerse as to identify) a white cloth in some red dye. This means that they would dip the white cloth in the red dye until the entire cloth was immersed or saturated with the red dye. The once white cloth is now the same color as the red dye; thus, identified with the red dye. Let's now consider what the Christian water baptism symbolizes.

8.0 The command to baptize is exclusively found in Matthew 28:19. Read this passage and answer the following questions:

    a. **To whom is the command to baptize given? How does this apply today?**

    b. **An example of baptism is found in Acts 8:36-39. What is the substance that Philip baptized his disciple (i.e. the Ethiopian eunuch)?**

    c. **One of the important truths baptism demonstrates is identification. With whom is the believer that is being baptized to be identified (i.e. who are they baptized into)?**

Session 11: *The Ordinances*

d. The biblical mode of Christian symbolic water baptism is trine immersion (dipping an individual three times). What substance is the future disciple dipped in that symbolically represents God the Father?

e. What substance is the future disciple dipped in that symbolically represents God the Son?

f. What substance symbolically represents God the Holy Spirit?

g. How many total dips are there? How many total baptisms?

h. How does letter "c" through "g" picture the Trinity (i.e. Persons of the Godhead as well as the Deity of each Person. Note: you may want to refer to the following article and chart to help answer this question)?

i. What is Christ commanding the church to do to all the people throughout the world in Matthew 28:16-20 (this command is commonly called the Great Commission)?

j. What are the three things a person is commanded to do in order to make disciples?

Session 11: *The Ordinances*

     In the baptism ordinance, each dip symbolically represents the identification of both the Deity and Personhood of each Person in the Godhead – God the Father, God the Son, and God the Holy Spirit. One of the three persons of the Godhead is God the Father. The substance that represents the essence, or Deity, of God the Father is H_2O. The first dip represents His Personhood. God the Father is distinct in person from the other two Persons of the Godhead (i.e. subsistence) but is the same in essence (i.e. substance). Another Person in the Godhead is God the Son; that is, Jesus Christ. The substance that represents the essence, or Deity, of God the Son is H_2O; the exact same substance as God the Father. He is the exact same in substance or essence as God the Father, but different in subsistence. The second dip represents God the Son's unique Personhood. God the Son is distinct in person from the other two Persons of the Godhead (i.e. subsistence) but is the same in essence (i.e. substance). And finally, the other Person in the Godhead is the Holy Spirit. The substance that represents the essence, or Deity, of God the Holy Spirit is H_2O; the exact same substance as God the Father and God the Son. He is the exact same in substance or essence as God the Father and God the Son. The third dip represents God the Holy Spirit's distinct Personhood. God the Holy Spirit is distinct in person from the other two Persons of the Godhead (i.e. subsistence) but is the same in essence (i.e. substance). Each dip in the baptismal formula represents both the Deity (i.e. substance or essence as represented by H_2O) of God the Father, of God the Son, and of God the Holy Spirit, as well as the uniqueness of all three Persons in the Godhead (i.e. as represented by the three separate dips). Though there are three dips in the baptism ordinance, the act of one complete baptism consisting of three dips symbolically represents the unity and oneness of God. There is but only one true God as there is only one complete baptism.

Session 11: *The Ordinances*

An ordinance has physical materials or actions that are commanded to be used and performed. These physical materials and/or actions are called elements. Each element within an ordinance symbolically represents a spiritual truth or reality. The following chart shows the relationship between the elements, what they symbolically represent, and the spiritual reality of the Baptism ordinance.

element/ physical action	↔ symbolic representation ↔	spiritual reality
Water	The Name of God (i.e. essence of God)	The Baptism ordinance pictures the immersion or identification of the child of God with the one true living and holy God existing eternally as three Persons (i.e. God the Father, God the Son, and God the Holy Spirit), through the rebirth by the gift of faith; and that this union and fellowship with God only exist through the finished work of Jesus Christ as He continues His ministry glorifying God by revealing His Name through His body (i.e. the God-ordained institution
The three dips into water	The Deity and Persons in the Godhead – God the Father, God the Son, and God the Holy Spirit	
One complete act of baptism	The unity and oneness of God	
The person baptizing (the discipler)	The God-ordained institution of the functioning church	
The person being baptized (the disciple)	The child of God submissive to God's salvation message and to the God-ordained institution of authority (i.e. the functioning church)	

Session 11: *The Ordinances*

notes

Session 12: *The Second Coming*

> **The Second Coming:** the personal, visible, and imminent return of Christ to gather His Church from the earth (1 Thessalonians 4:16-17); His return will be before the seven year tribulation (1 Thessalonians 1:10; Revelations 3:10); and afterward to descend with the Church to establish His millennial kingdom upon the earth (Rev. 19:11-20:6).

1.0 **Look up the word "imminent" in a dictionary and write down some key words of the definition.**

2.0 **Read 1 Thessalonians 5:1-11 and answer the following questions:**

v. 2. The "day of the Lord" refers to the imminent return of Christ. How is Christ's imminent return described here?

v. 3. Describe the world's attitude at the time of Christ's return.

v. 4. Will Jesus' return be "like a thief in the night" for believers? Why or why not?

vv. 6-8. Since Christians may be caught up together with Jesus at any moment (1 Thessalonians 4:15-17), how should that affect the way we live?

Session 12: *The Second Coming*

v. 9. What has God appointed for unbelievers? What has God appointed for believers?

v. 10. Whether believers are alive or dead (i.e. asleep), what has Christ's death done for believers?

v. 11. What should believers do with the above knowledge?

The Bible teaches that prior to the establishment of Christ's 1,000-year kingdom (i.e. millennial kingdom), the world will experience seven years of tribulation. The Tribulation period will be preceded by Christ's taking up His Church (i.e. the rapture), which includes both the living and the dead in Christ. While Christ and His bride are in heaven, God punishes the wickedness of man during the Tribulation. This period culminates with the battle of Armageddon when Christ returns to earth with His heavenly armies to conquer the armies of earth (Revelation 19:11-21), bind Satan and his angels (Revelation 20:1-3), and establish His millennial Kingdom (Revelation 20:4-6).

The events of the seven-year Tribulation are found in Revelation chapters 6 – 19. There are three sets of supernatural, horrible judgments: the seven seal judgments, the seven trumpet judgments, and the seven bowl judgments. Reading through these chapters can be a very terrifying experience for those who do not know Christ. However, there is good news for the Christian.

Session 12: *The Second Coming*

Three Views of the Rapture

There are three primary interpretations of when Jesus will return for His Church (an event commonly called the Rapture, 1 Thessalonians 4:16-17).

Pretribulational View: Rapture occurs before the Tribulation

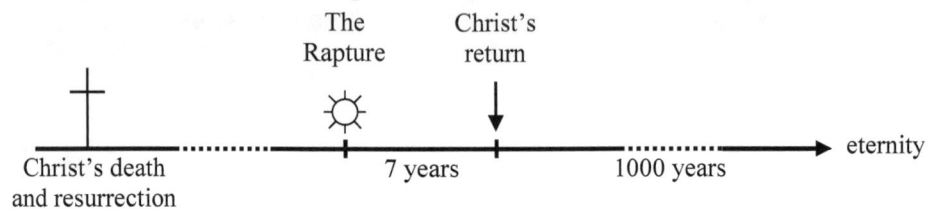

```
                    The         Christ's
                  Rapture       return
     †              ☼             ↓
  ───┼────────────┼─────────────┼──────────────▶ eternity
  Christ's death    7 years        1000 years
  and resurrection
```

Midtribulational View: Rapture occurs in the midst of the Tribulation

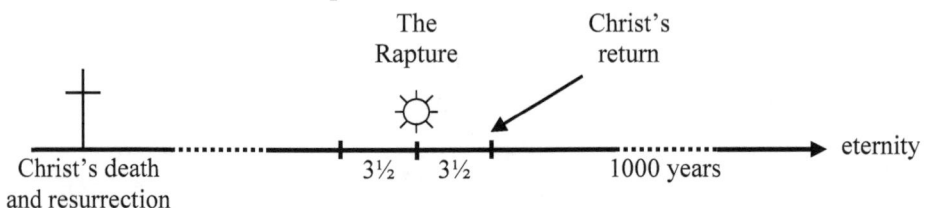

```
                          The         Christ's
                        Rapture       return
     †                    ☼              ↙
  ───┼──────────────────┼────┼─────────────┼──────▶ eternity
  Christ's death        3½    3½           1000 years
  and resurrection
```

Posttribulational View: Rapture occurs after the Tribulation

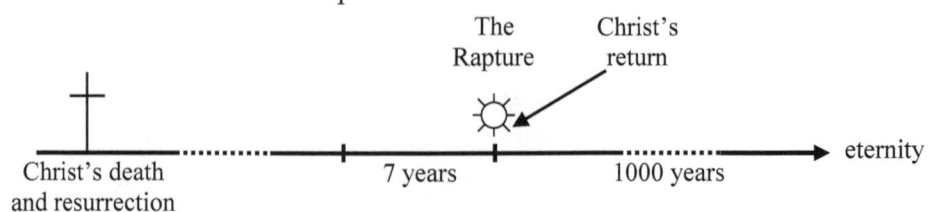

```
                                 The      Christ's
                               Rapture    return
     †                           ☼ ↙
  ───┼───────────────────────┼────┼──────────────▶ eternity
  Christ's death             7 years       1000 years
  and resurrection
```

Session 12: *The Second Coming*

3.1 **What is promised concerning God's people and the wrath of God in each of the following passages?**

Daniel 12:1 -

1 Thessalonians 1:10 -

1 Thessalonians 5:9 -

Revelation 3:10 -

3.2 **Which view of the rapture (i.e. when Christ will return for His Church) is most consistent with the above promises?**

❑ **Pretribulation (often called Pre-trib;** i.e. the rapture occurs before the tribulation)
❑ **Midtribulation (often called mid-trib;** i.e. the rapture occurs in the midst of the tribulation)
❑ **Posttribulation (often called post-trib;** i.e. the rapture occurs after the tribulation)

4.0 **Describe the events that will take place at the Rapture (1 Corinthians 15:51-52 and 1 Thessalonians 4:16-17).**

5.0 **According to Matthew 24:27-30 and Revelation 1:7, who will witness Christ's return?**

Session 12: *The Second Coming*

6.0 How long will the millennial kingdom last (Revelation 20:1-7)?

7.0 Who will rule in the millennial kingdom (Matthew 19:27-30 and 1 Corinthians 6:2)?

    A popular eschatological doctrine (i.e. end-times teaching) that has gained popularity near the end of the twentieth century is the Prewrath rapture. The prewrath position emphasizes the biblical distinction between tribulation (which Christians have been promised) and the wrath of God (which Christians have been promised deliverance/salvation from). The idea is that Christians will be raptured sometime between the beginning of the great tribulation, but before the day of the Lord's wrath (i.e. sometime during the second half of the seventieth week of Daniel).

    Some believers think there will be no literal 1,000-year kingdom (amillennial view) while others believe the we are presently in the kingdom era (postmillennial view). The premillennial view understands that Christ will return with His saints to rule over the world for a literal 1,000 years. Much of the confusion relating to the Millennial Kingdom is due to interpreting the prophecies for Israel as being symbolic and being fulfilled through the Church, rather than taking a literal interpretation and seeing a distinction between Israel and the Church.

    "Premillennialist [and Pretribulationalist] take both history and prophecy literally... just as in any proper interpretation of Old Testament history, Joseph is always Joseph and not Christ, even so in prophesy Israel is always Israel and never the Church."[5]

---

[5] Dr. Alva J. McClain, Founder of Grace Theological Seminary

Session 12: *The Second Coming*

notes

Session 13: *The Future Life*

> **The Future Life:** the conscious existence of the dead (Philippians 1:21-23; Luke 16:19-31); the resurrection of the body (John 5:28-29); the judgment and reward of believers (Romans 14:10-12; 2 Corinthians 5:10); the judgment and condemnation of unbelievers (Revelation 20:11-15); the eternal life of the believers (John 3:16); and the eternal punishment of the unbelievers (Matthew 25:46; Revelation 20:15).

1.0 What does the Bible reveal about the relationship between the body and the spirit in Luke 23:46; Acts 7:59-60; and James 2:26?

2.0 Read Luke 16:19-31. Answer the following questions:

vv. 19-21. Who are the two characters of this biblical account?

vv. 22-23. Where did each of the two characters go when they died?

v. 24. What did the rich man request of Abraham and why?

vv. 25-26. Why did Abraham say that Lazarus could not do what the rich man requested?

vv. 27-28. What was the second request of the rich man?

v. 29. What did Abraham say was the solution for the rich man's five brothers?

vv. 30-31. How was Abraham's statement to the rich man true for today's society as well?

Session 13: *The Future Life*

3.0 According to Revelation 20:11-15, who is judged at the white throne judgment and why will they enter into the second death?

4.0 According to John 3:16, what will people inherit that believe in the Lord Jesus Christ?

5.0 The Bible teaches that believers are saved on the basis of grace through faith in God's Word – not works. All the sins (past, present, and future sins) of believers have been forgiven on the basis of faith in Christ. According to Matthew 16:27; Romans 14:10-12; and 2 Corinthians 5:10:

   a. Who will judge believers (Hint: you may also want to refer to John 5:22; 5:30; 8:15-16; and 8:50)?

   b. What is it about the believer that will be judged?

   c. Where will this judgment take place?

   d. What will the believer receive at this judgment?

Session 13: *The Future Life*

6.0 1 Corinthians 3:10-15 creates a picture of the judgment which believers will experience (i.e. often this is called the bema judgment seat of Christ). In this passage, Christ is the foundation and the works of the believer are the building materials. Answer the following questions about the judgment to come for believers:

a. What do Christians receive at this judgment?

b. List works you would consider to be wood, hay, and straw.

c. List works you would consider to be gold, silver, and precious stones.

d. How is it possible that the same work performed by two Christians could be judged as a lasting work in one case (gold, silver, and precious stones) and a perishable work in the other (wood, hay, and straw)?

7.0 According to John 5:28-29 and 1 Corinthians 15:21-22:

a. Who will be resurrected?

b. When will believers be resurrected (Hint: you may want to refer to Session 12, question 2)?

c. When do you think unbelievers will be resurrected?

Session 13: *The Future Life*

8.0 In 1 Corinthians 15:42-49, Paul contrasts the believer's physical body with the glorified body that will be received at the resurrection. Write down some of these contrasts:

Verse	Earthly Body		Resurrected Body
42	_____	vs	_____
43	_____	vs	_____
44	_____	vs	_____
49	_____	vs	_____

9.0 According to 2 Corinthians 5:8-9 and Philippians 1:21-24:

a. what was Paul's attitude toward death?

b. what single principle governed how he lived his life?

c. is there any greater principle that should govern our lives?

Session 13: *The Future Life*

Place the correct corresponding letter on the appropriate line of the time line diagram on the following page (the first one is done for you).

- A. **Christ's First Coming.** His incarnation through virgin birth; His ministry, Death, Burial, Resurrection and Ascension.

- B. **Christ's Second Coming and The Judgment Seat of Christ** (i.e. bēma seat judgment). Christ will descend with the cry of command from an archangel and the trumpet sound of God. The dead in Christ will be raised and the present living believers will be caught up in the air with Him. Then all the saint's works will be judged and duly rewarded (1 Thessalonians 4:16-17; 2 Corinthians 5:10; 1 Cor 3:10-15).

- C. **Eternity** (Revelation 21:1-5).

- D. **The Battle of Armageddon.** The climactic battle between God and the adversary. The adversary, his demons, and all the deceived nations gathered to battle against the Lord are defeated. Satan is then bound for a thousand years (Revelation 16:14-16 and Revelation 20:1-3).

- E. **The Church Age.** This present age began at Pentecost and will end with the resurrection (i.e. rapture) of the Church (Acts 2:1-4 with 1 Thessalonians 4:16-17).

- F. **The Final Rebellion.** Satan is released and deceives the people. The rebellion is stopped and Satan is cast into the lake of fire (Revelation 20:7-10). The resurrection of unbelievers and the Great White throne judgment (Revelation 20:11-15). The creation of the new heaven and new earth (Revelation 21:1-4).

- G. **The Millennial Kingdom.** Christ and the saints rule the earth for a thousand years (Revelation 20:1-6).

- H. **The Tribulation.** The period commonly called the tribulation will last a total of 7 years. The first 3½ years will be peaceful. Then the two witness of God will be killed and lay dead for 3½ days. They will then be resurrected (Rev 11:1-13). The last 3½ years will be utterly miserable experiencing God's wrath.

Session 13: *The Future Life*

A

almost 2,000 years and counting

3½ years

3½ years

1,000

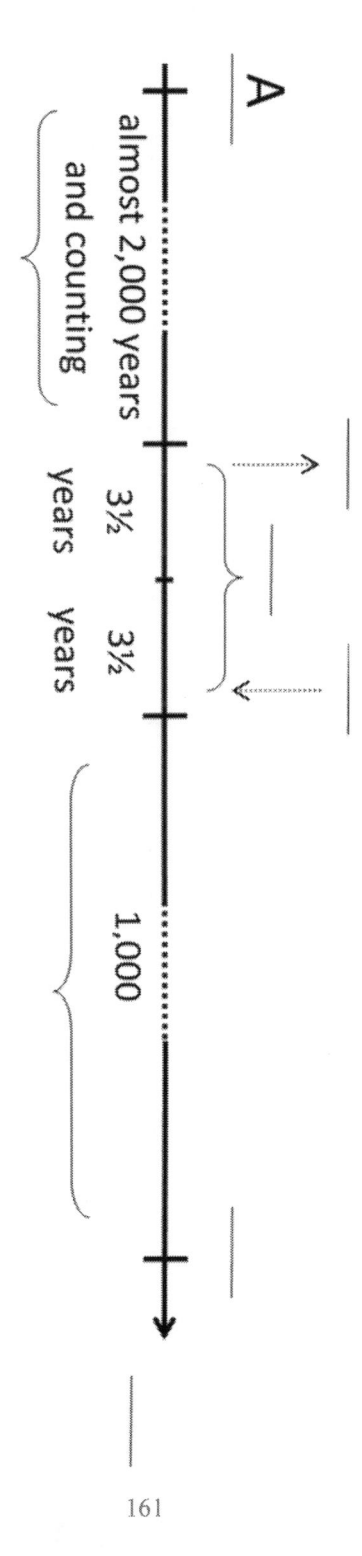

161

Made in the USA
Charleston, SC
05 March 2014